631ART.COM PRESENTS :

I0478017

"COSMIC INSPIRATION"

A COLORING BOOK

BY EDDIE ALFARO

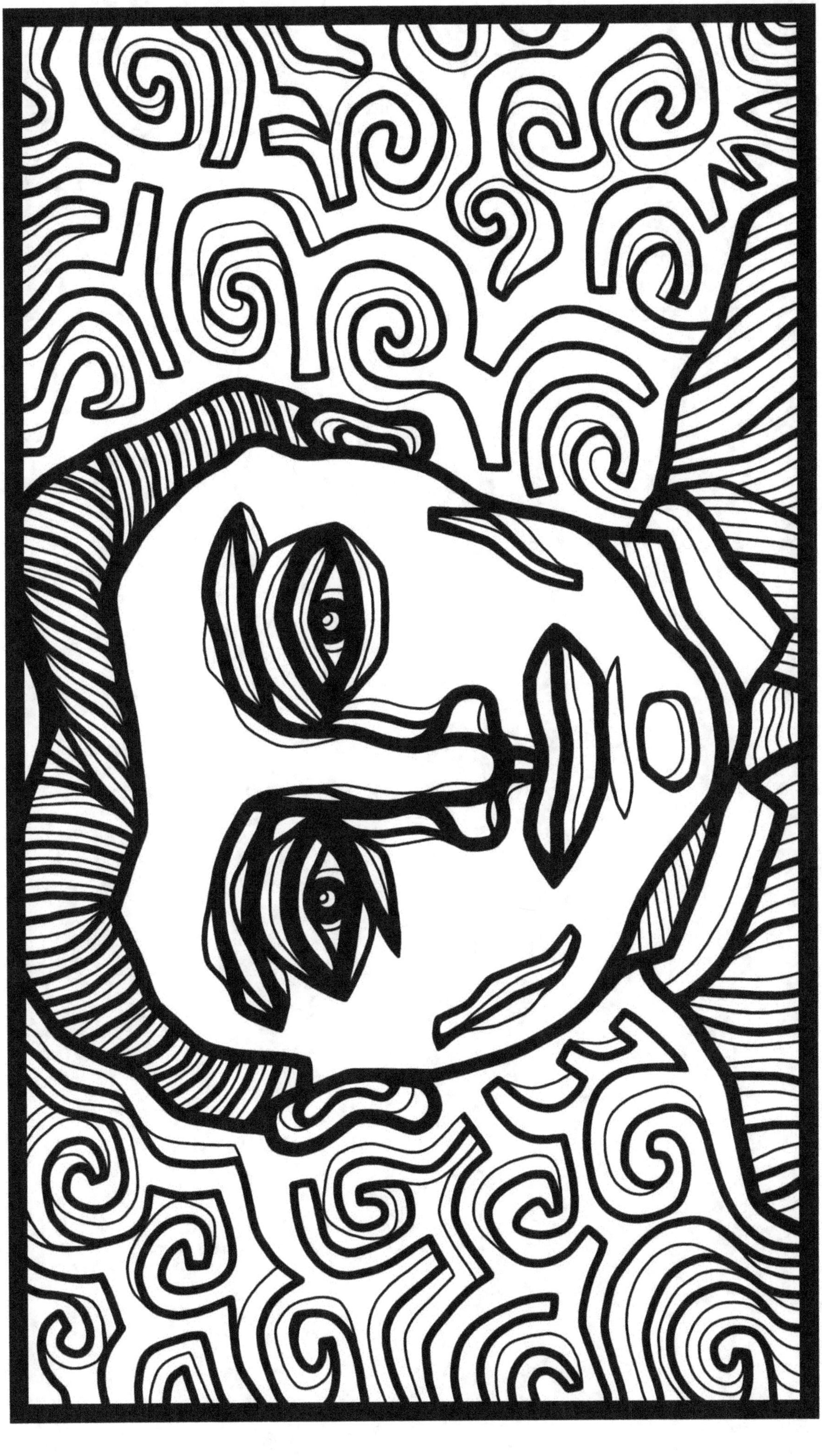

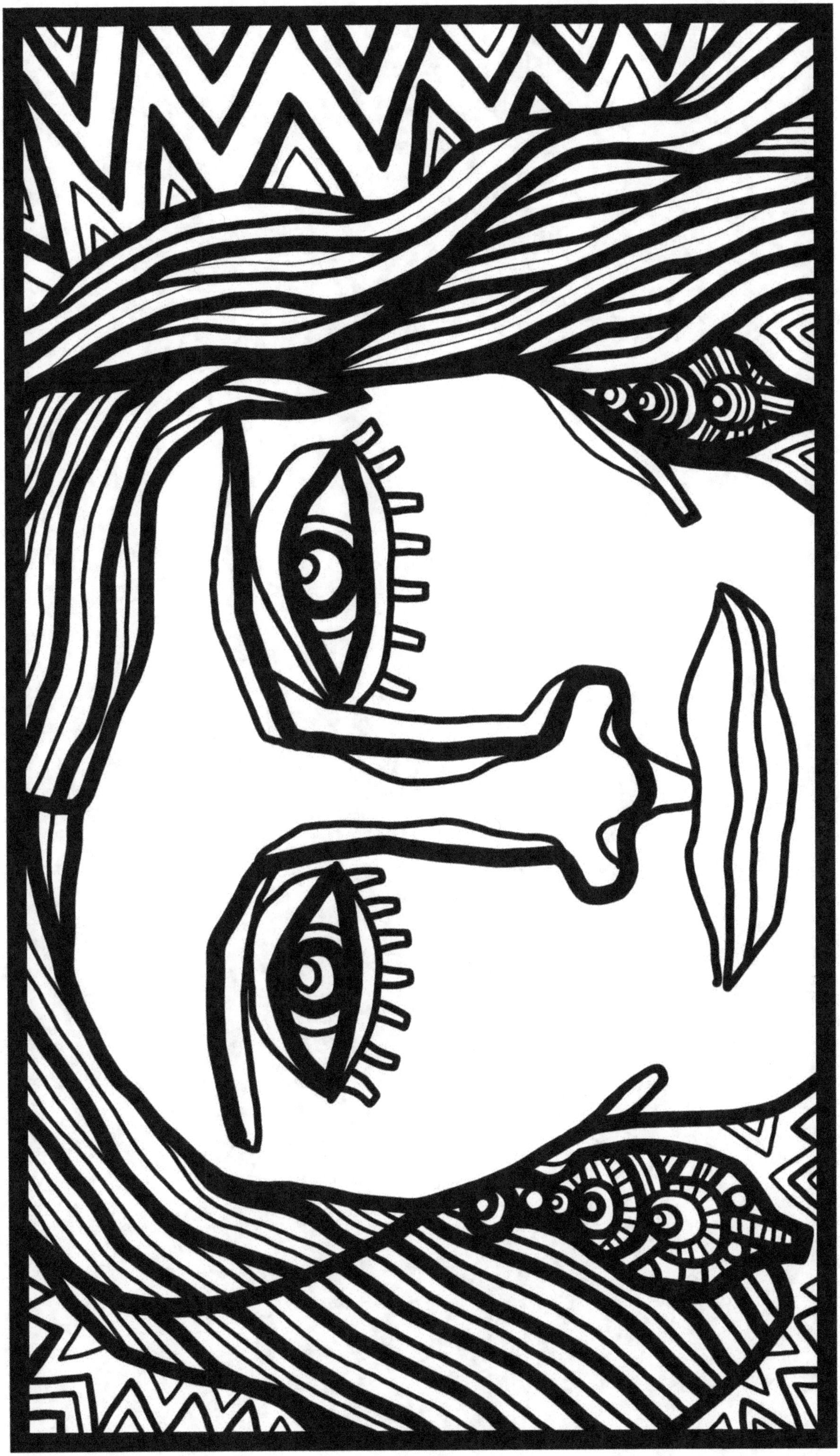

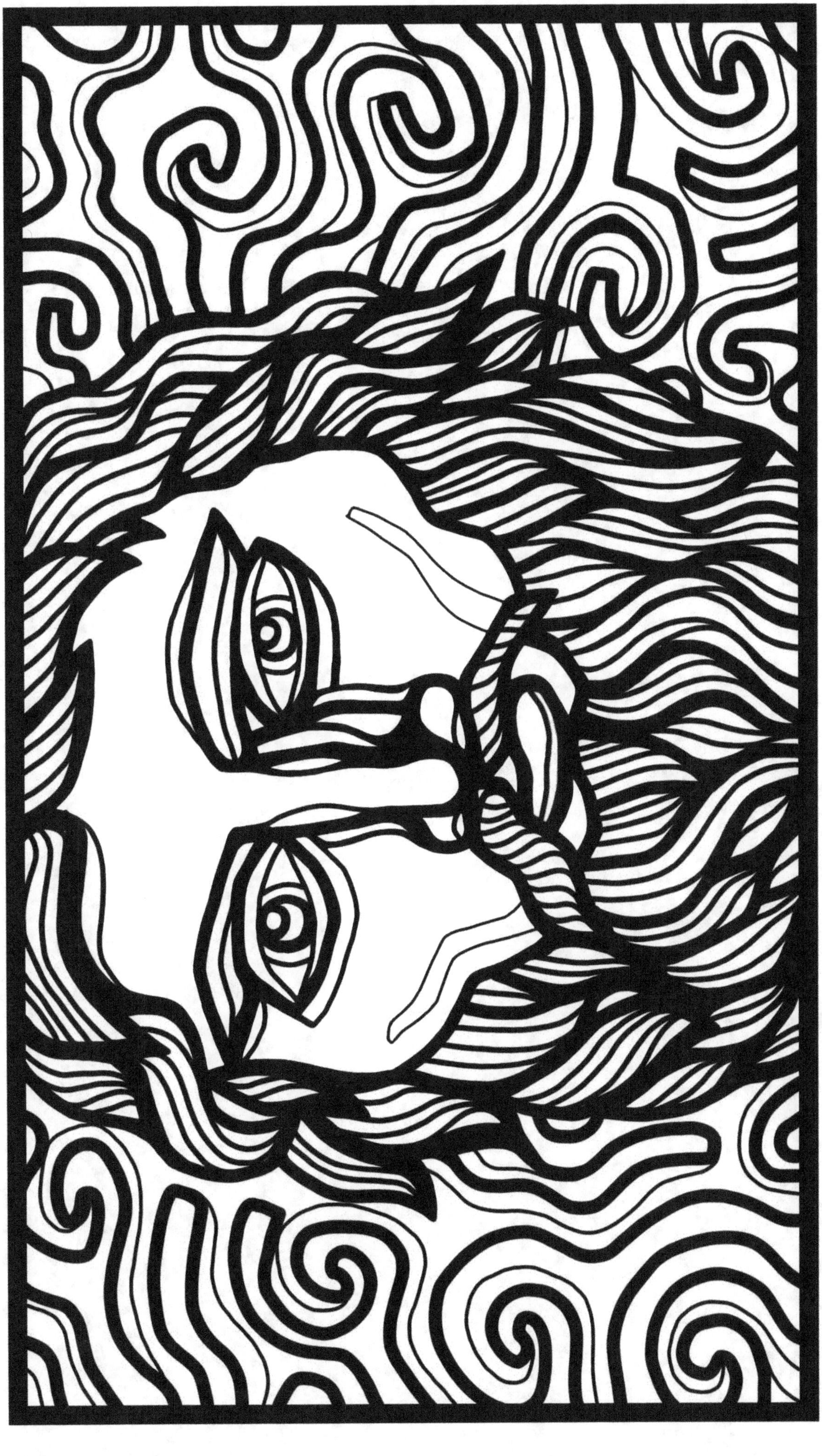

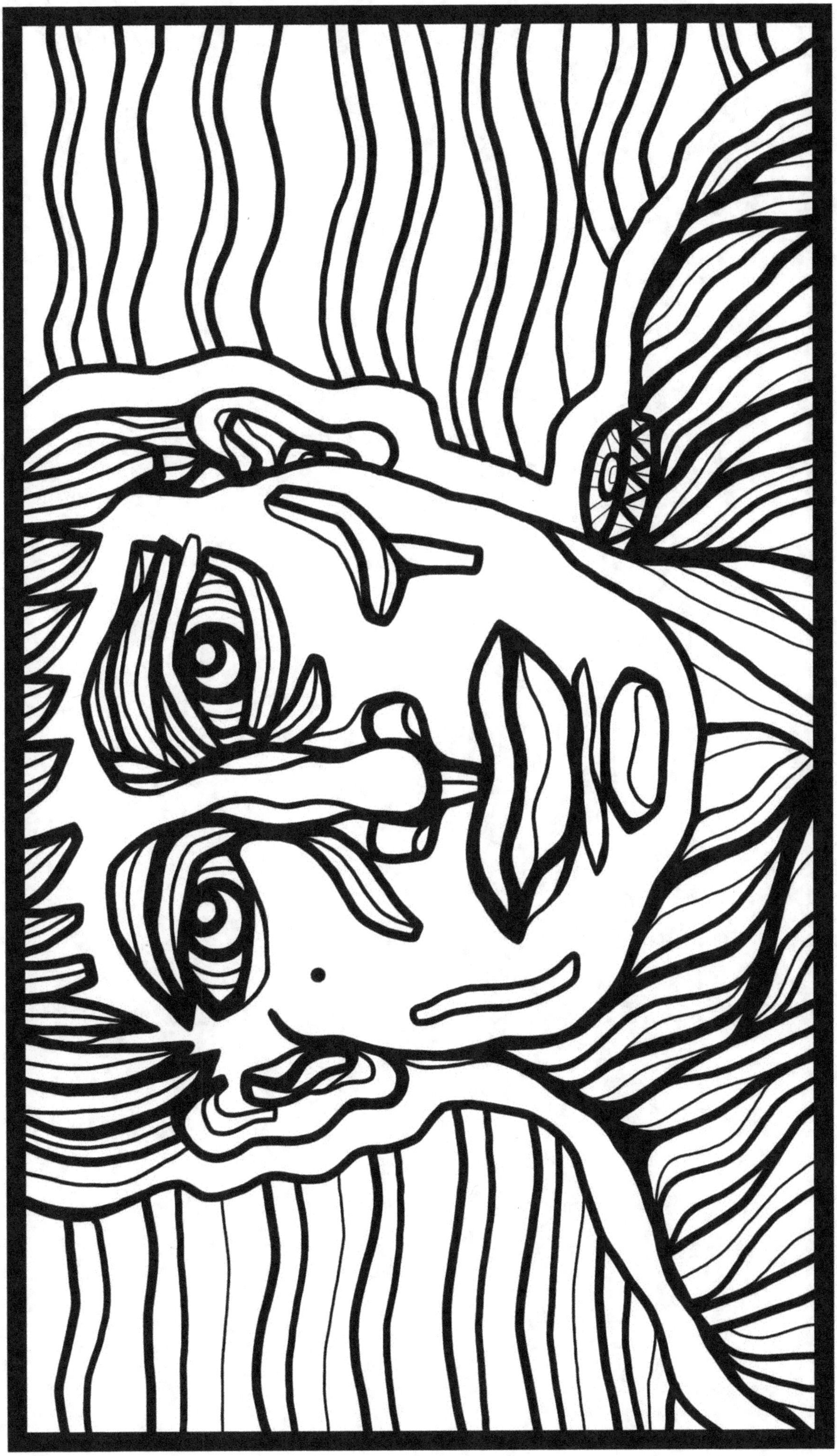

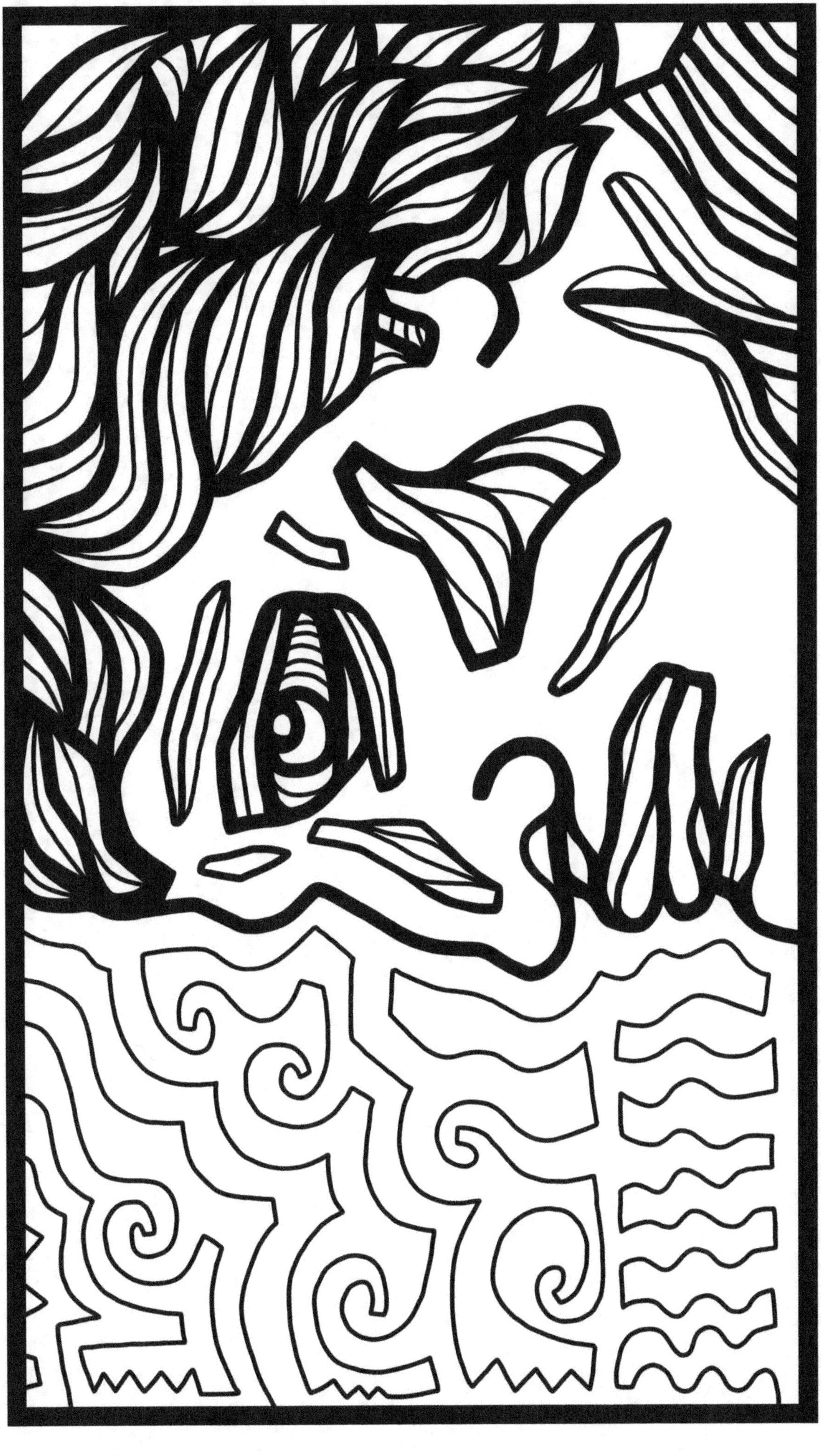

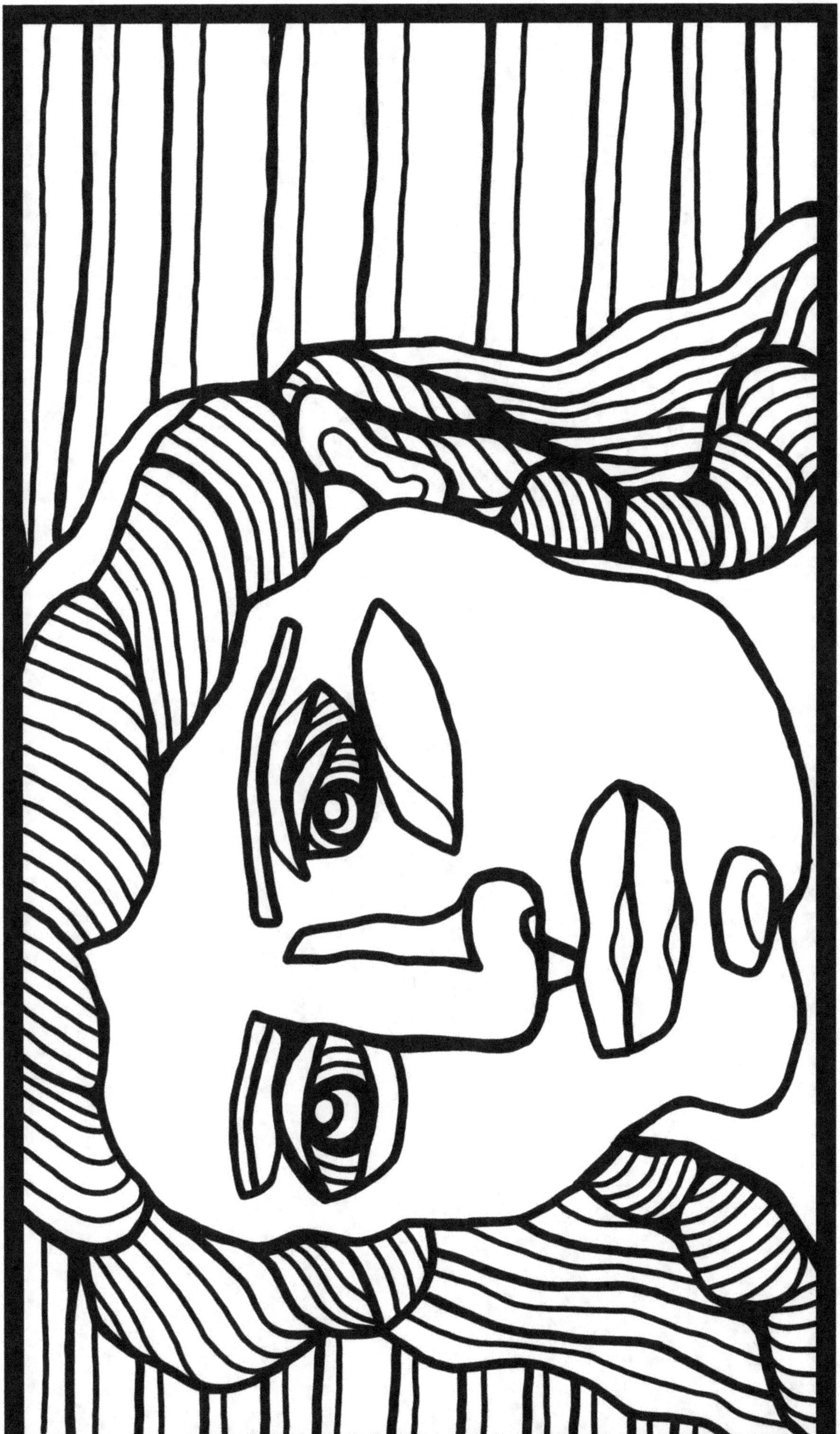

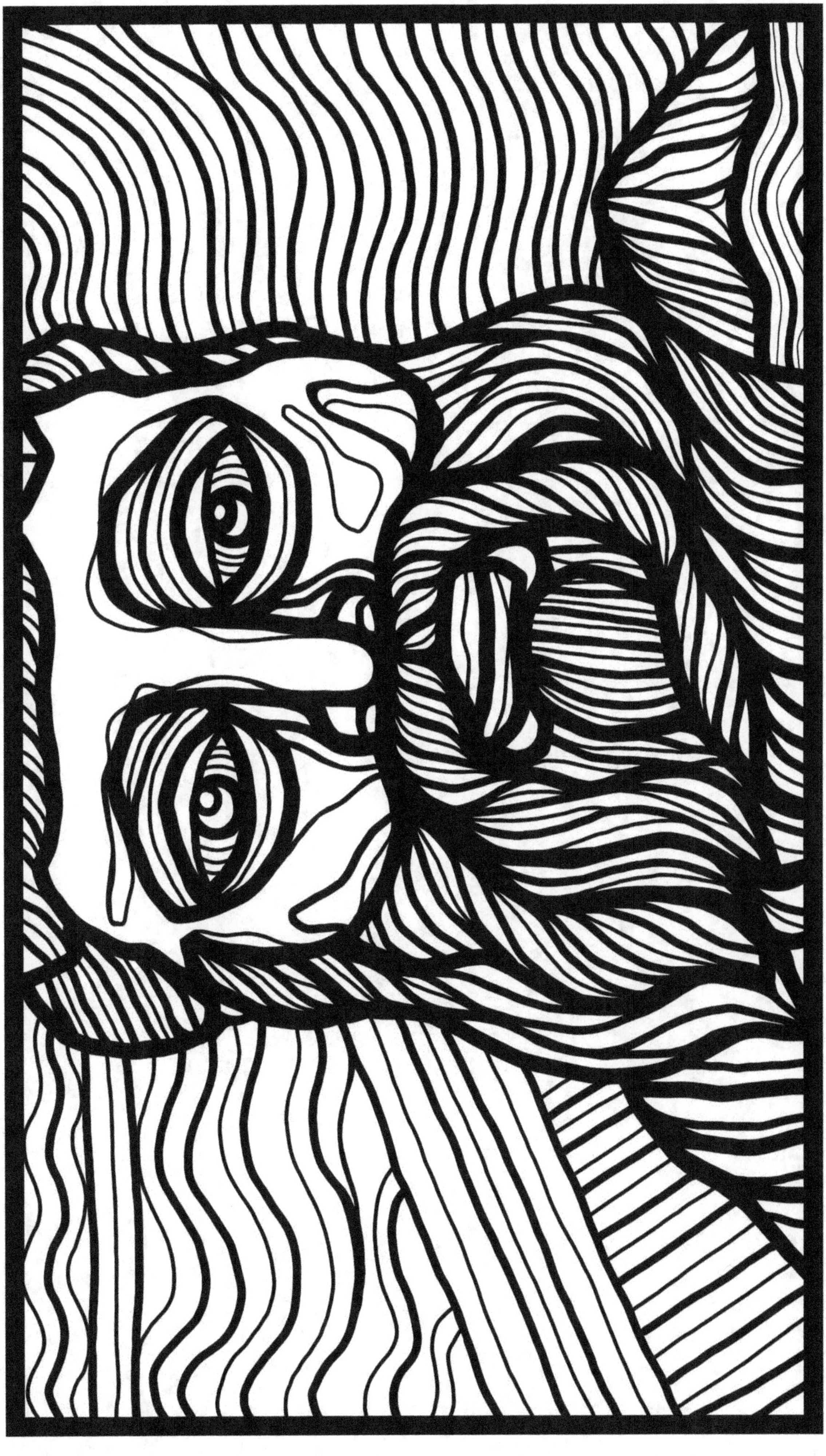

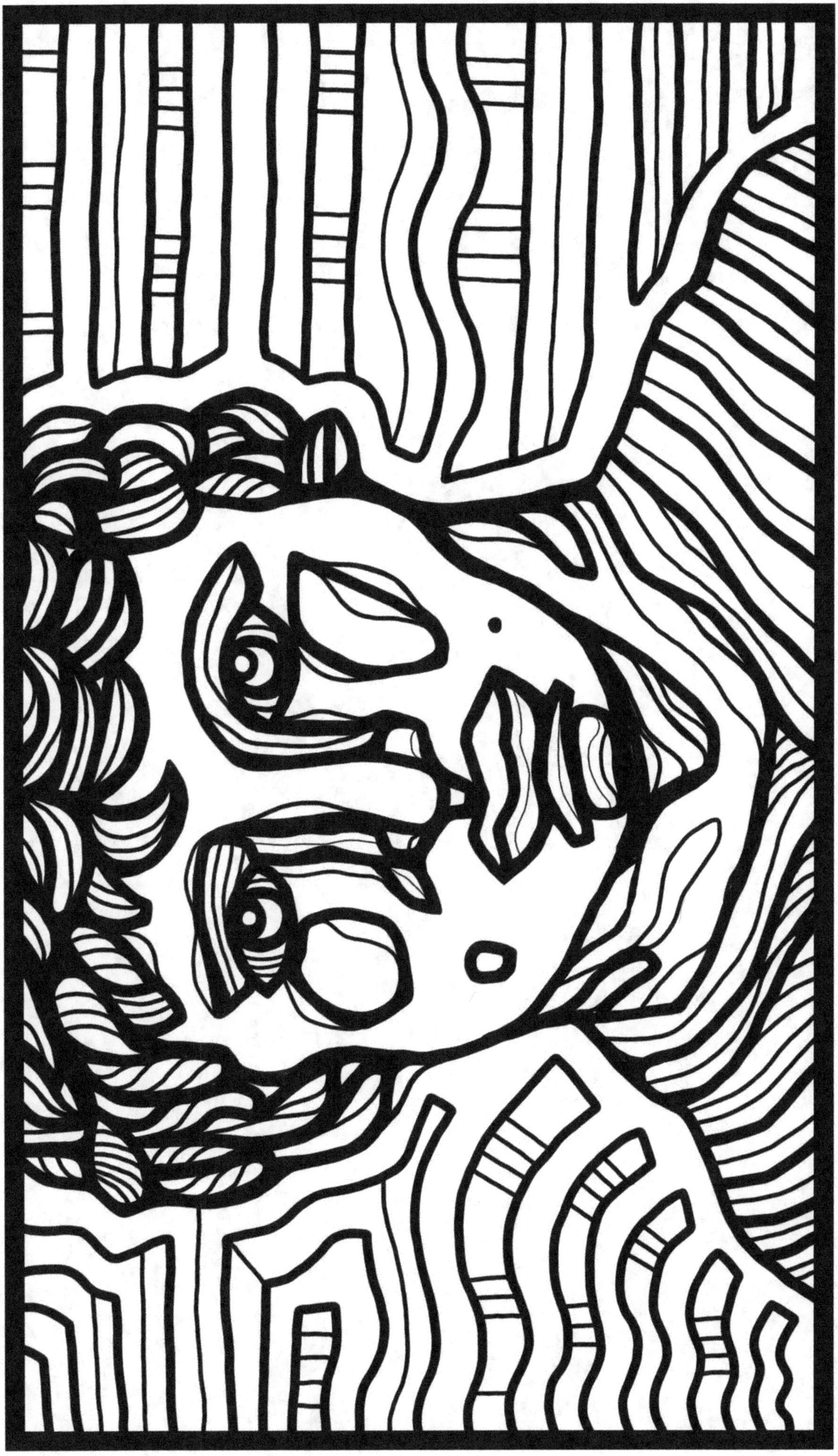

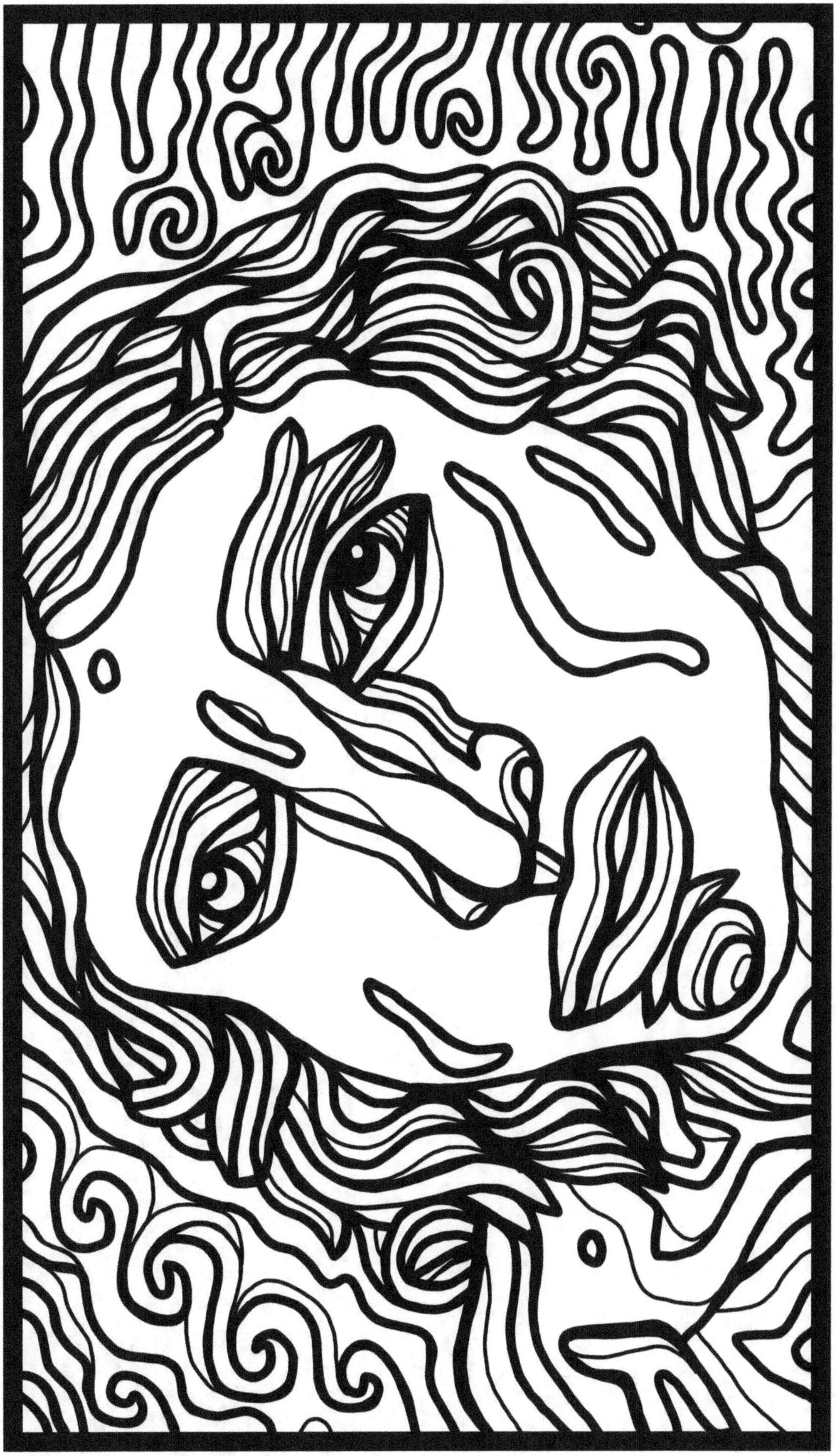

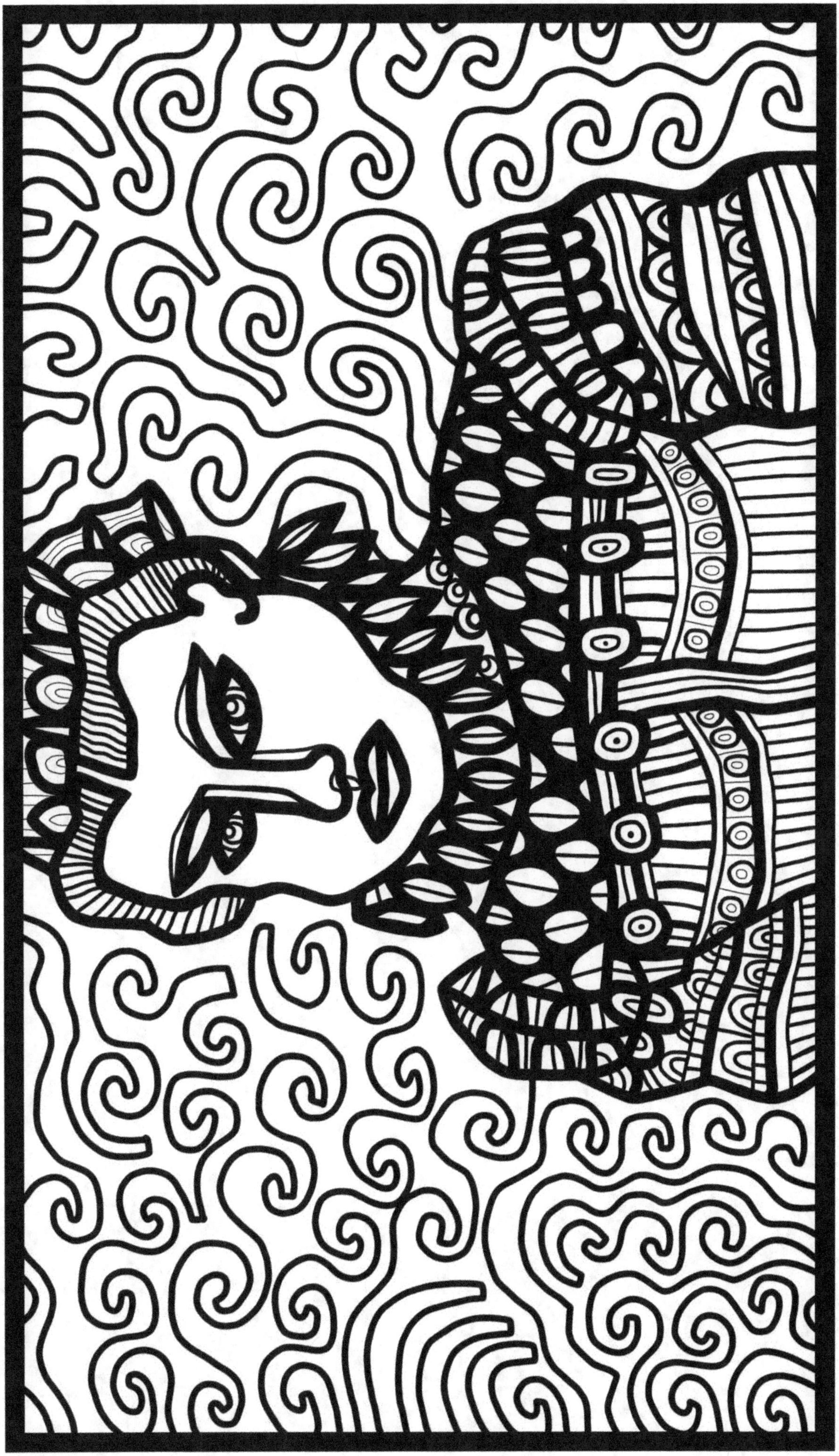

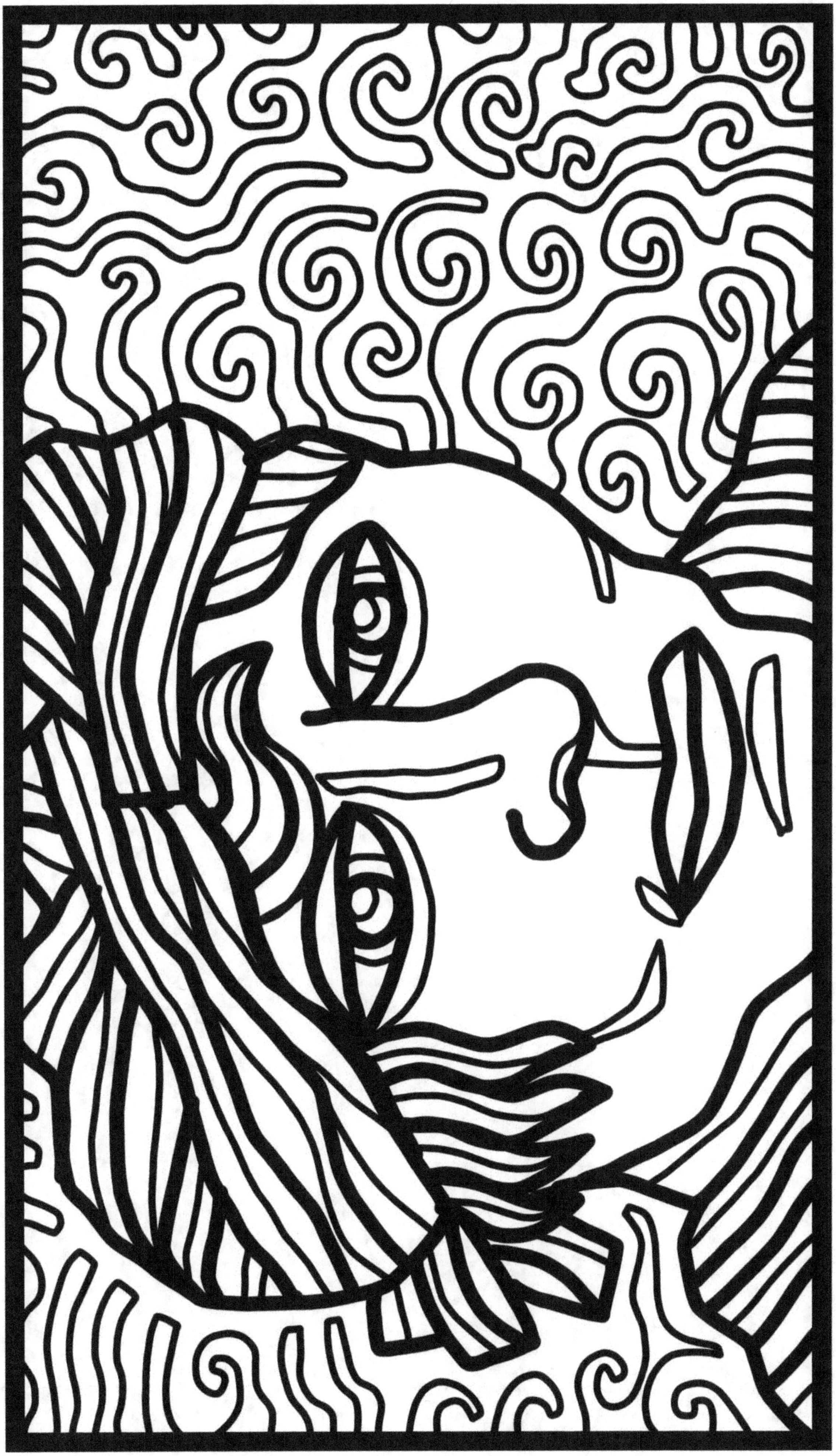

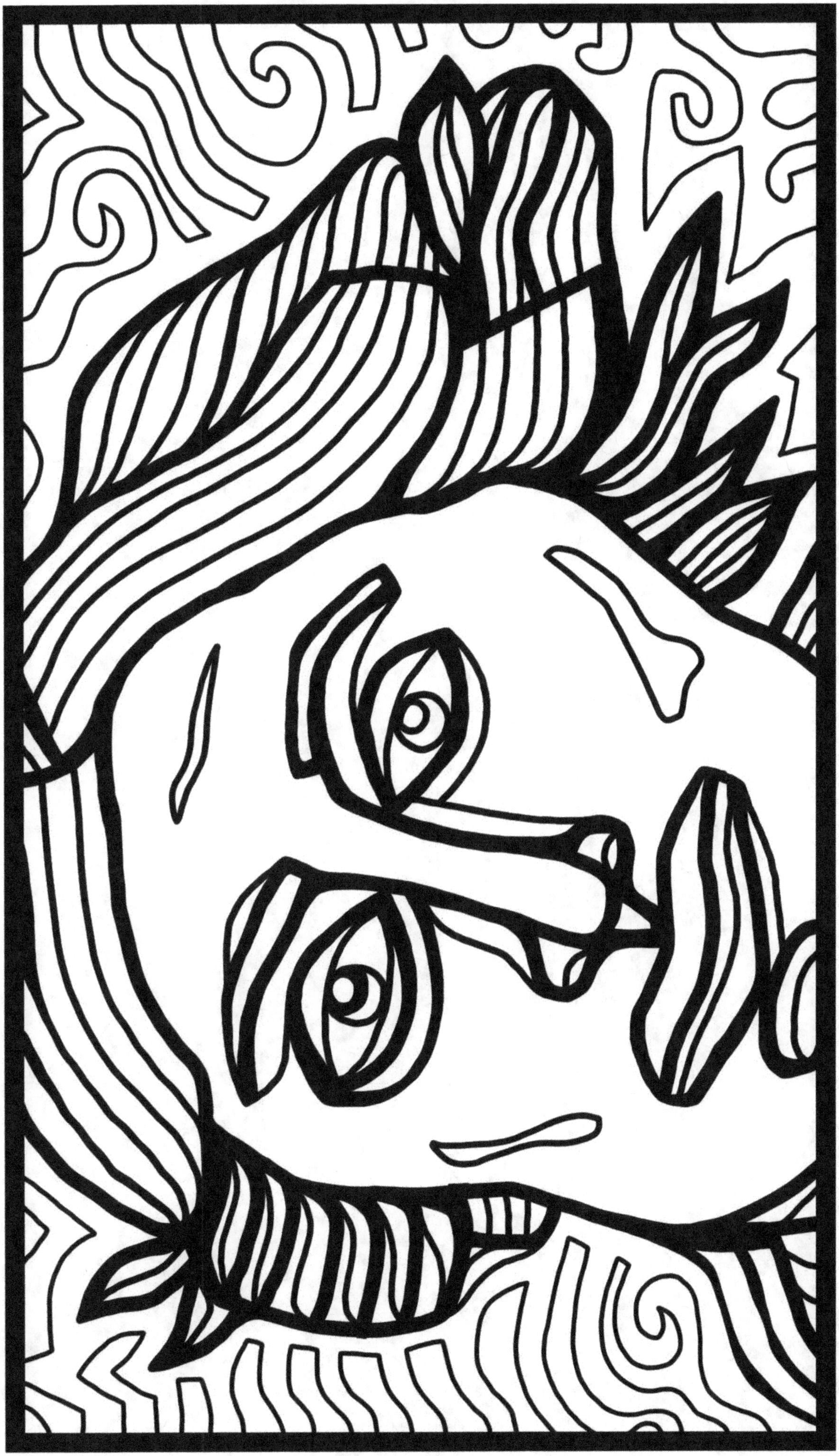

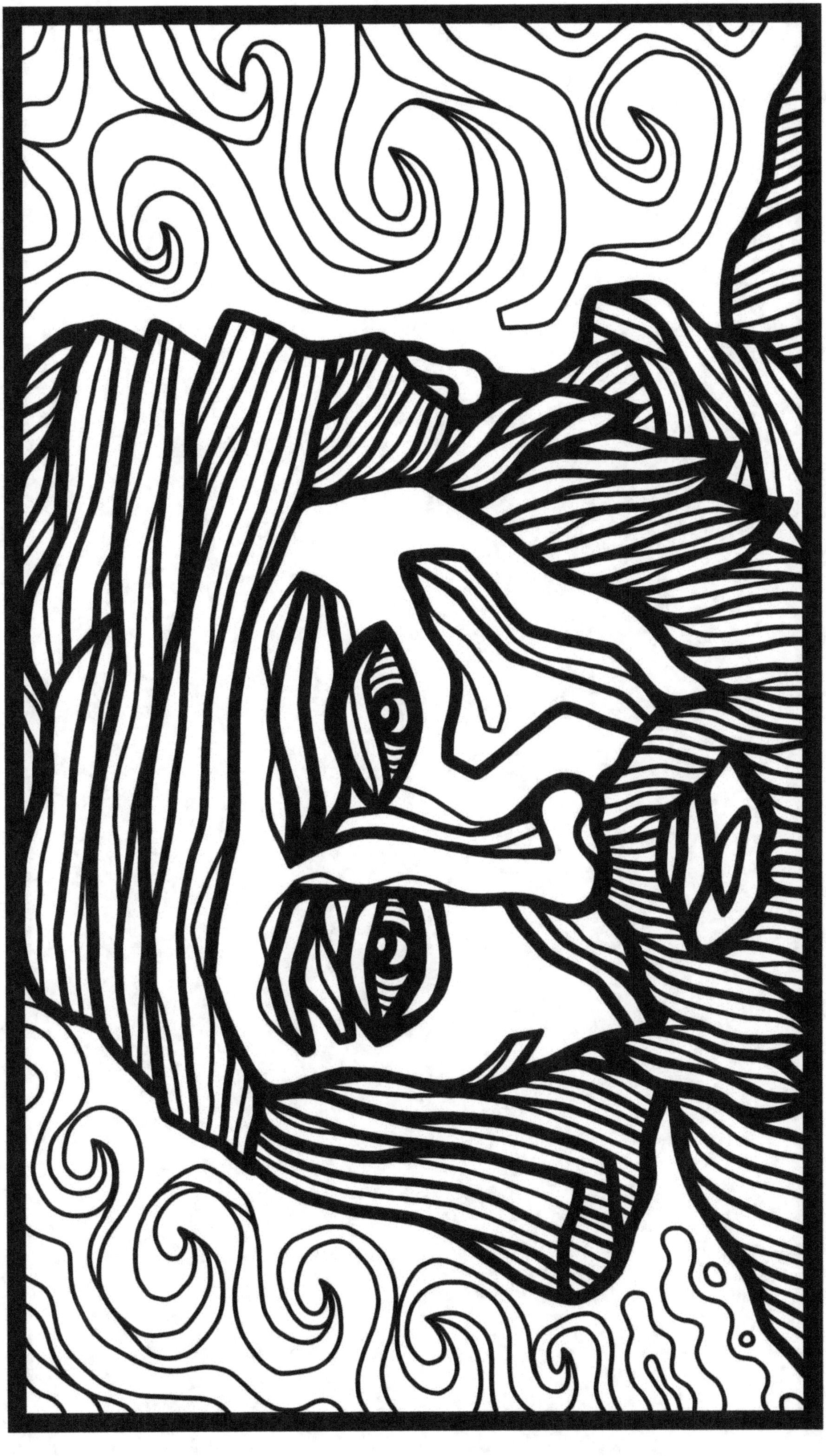

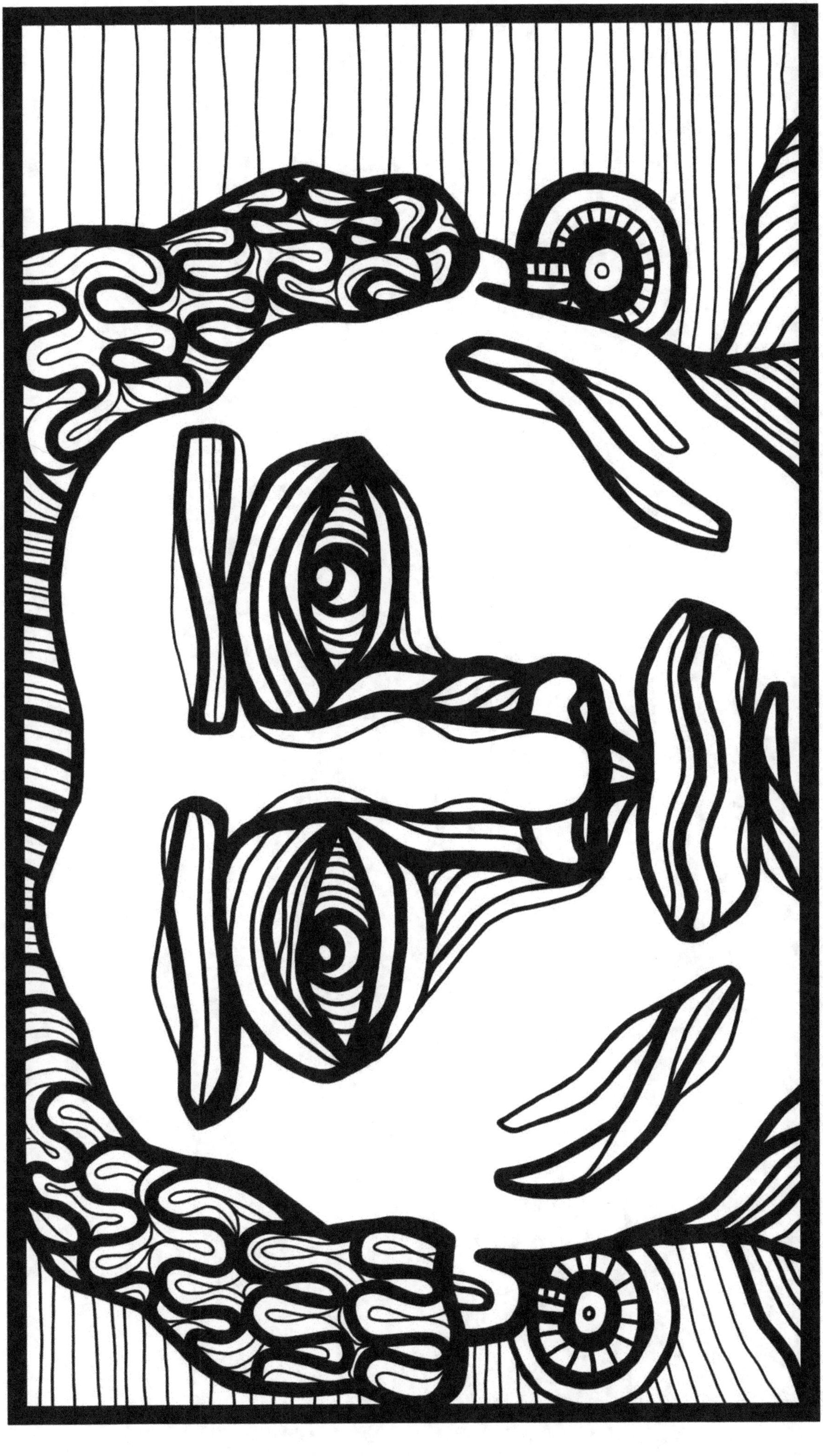

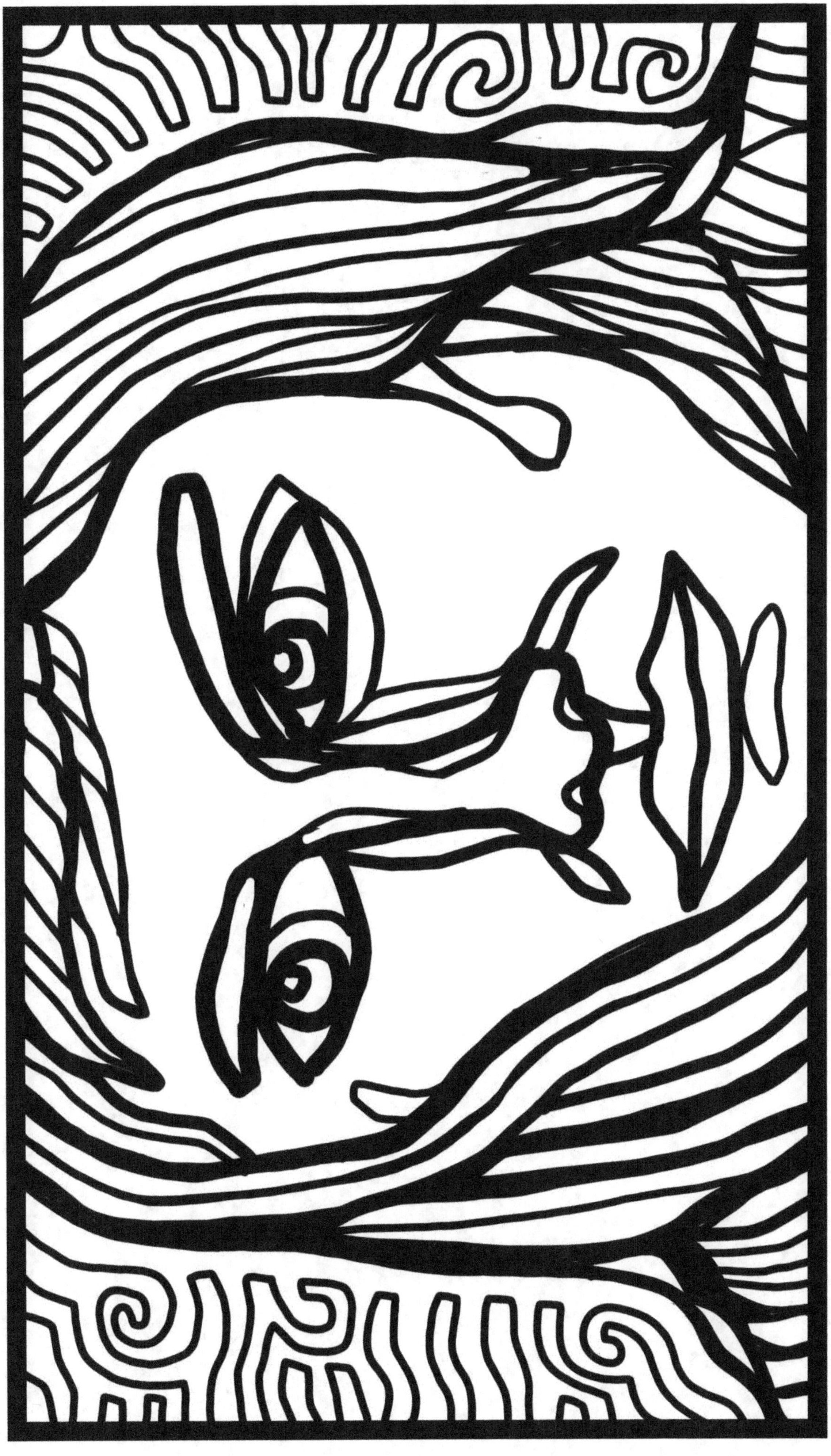

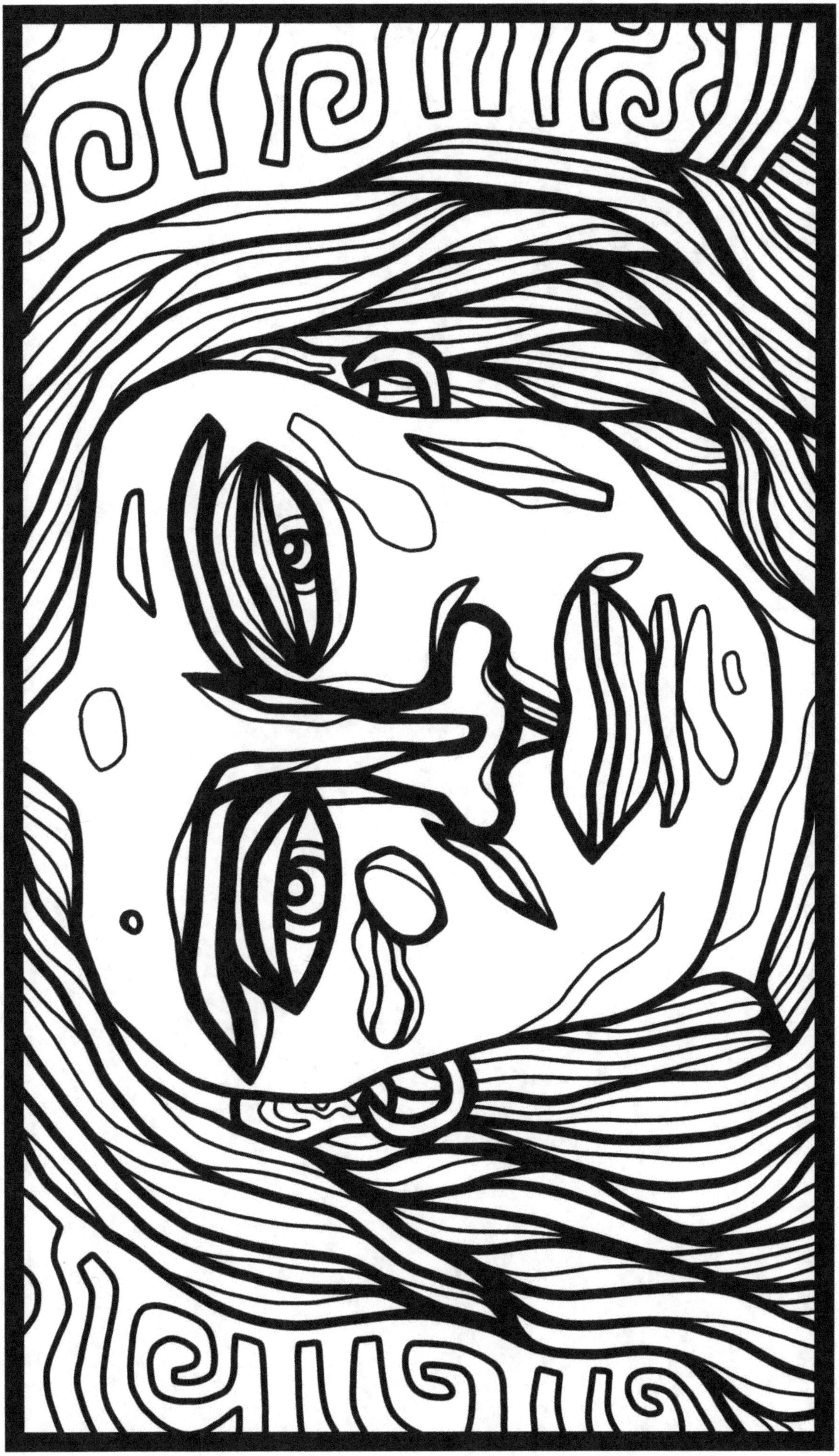

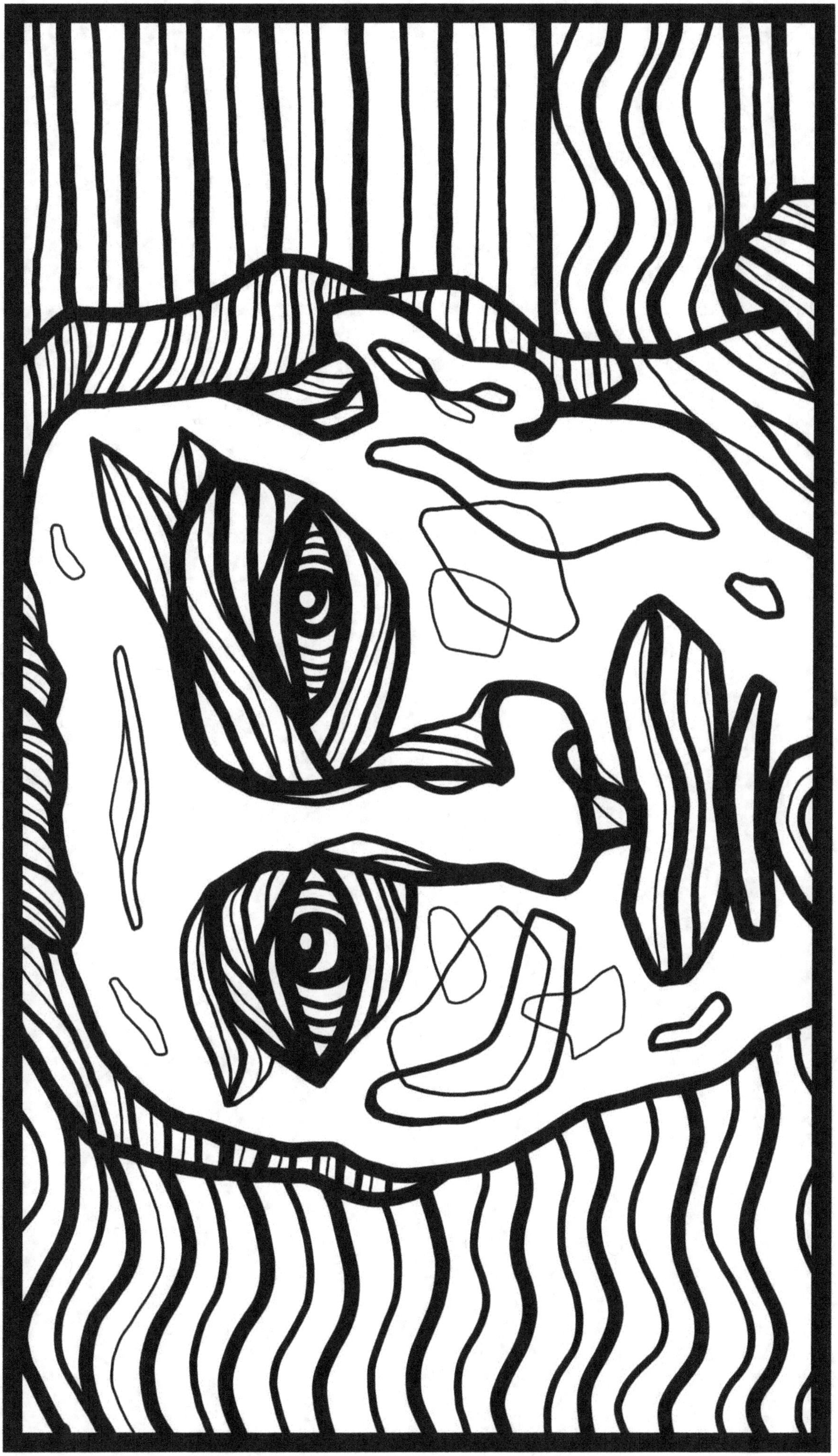

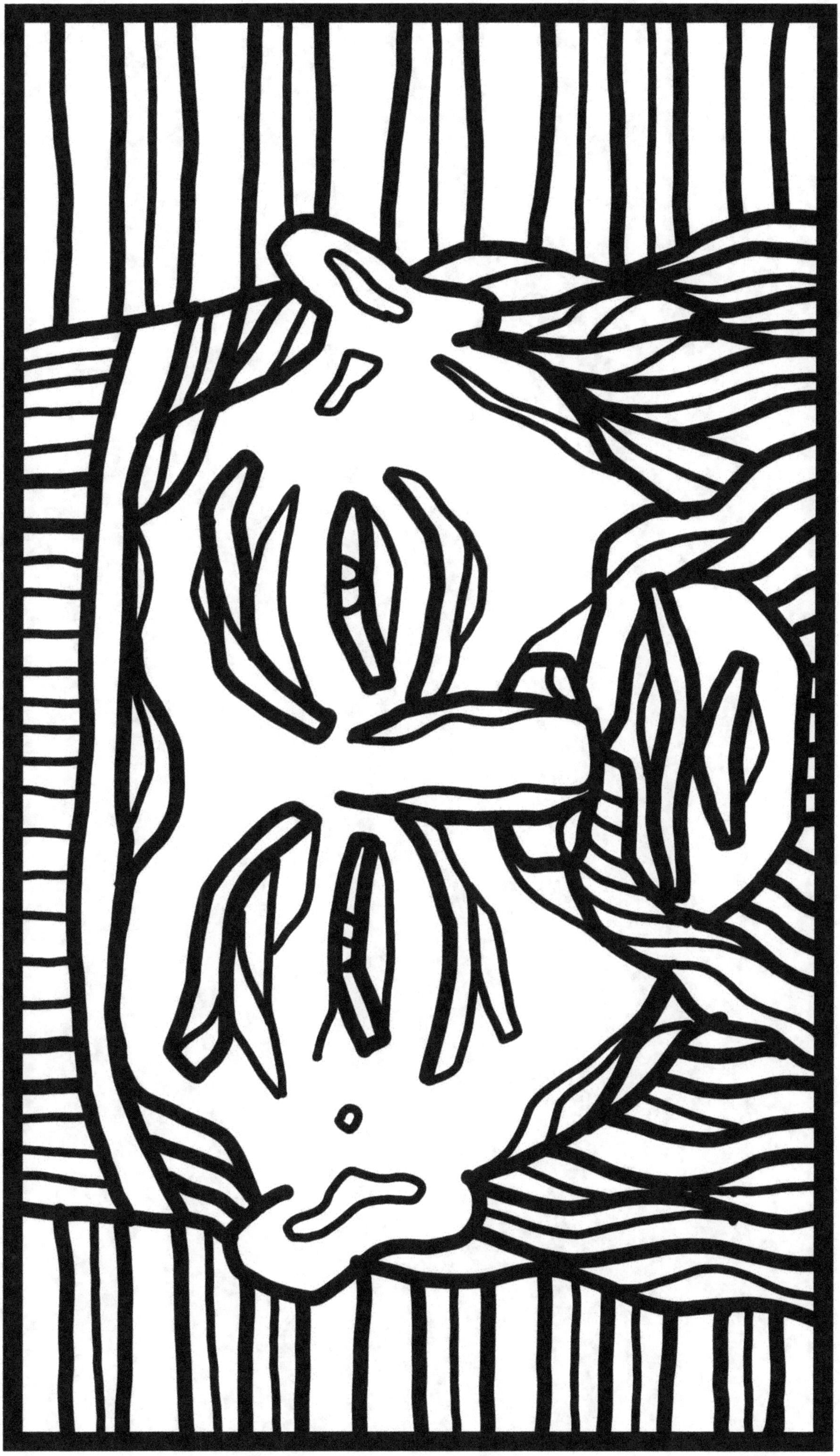

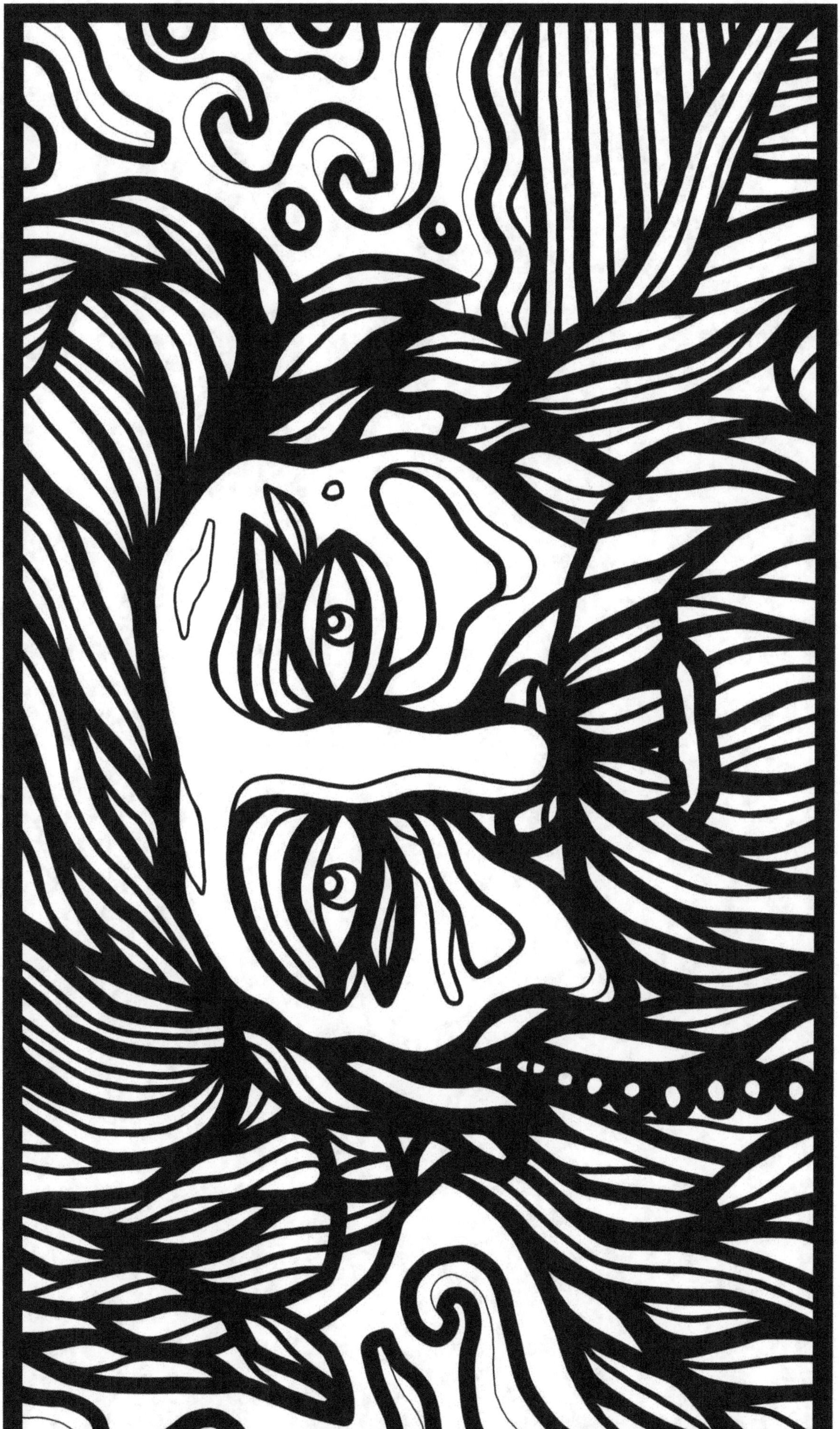

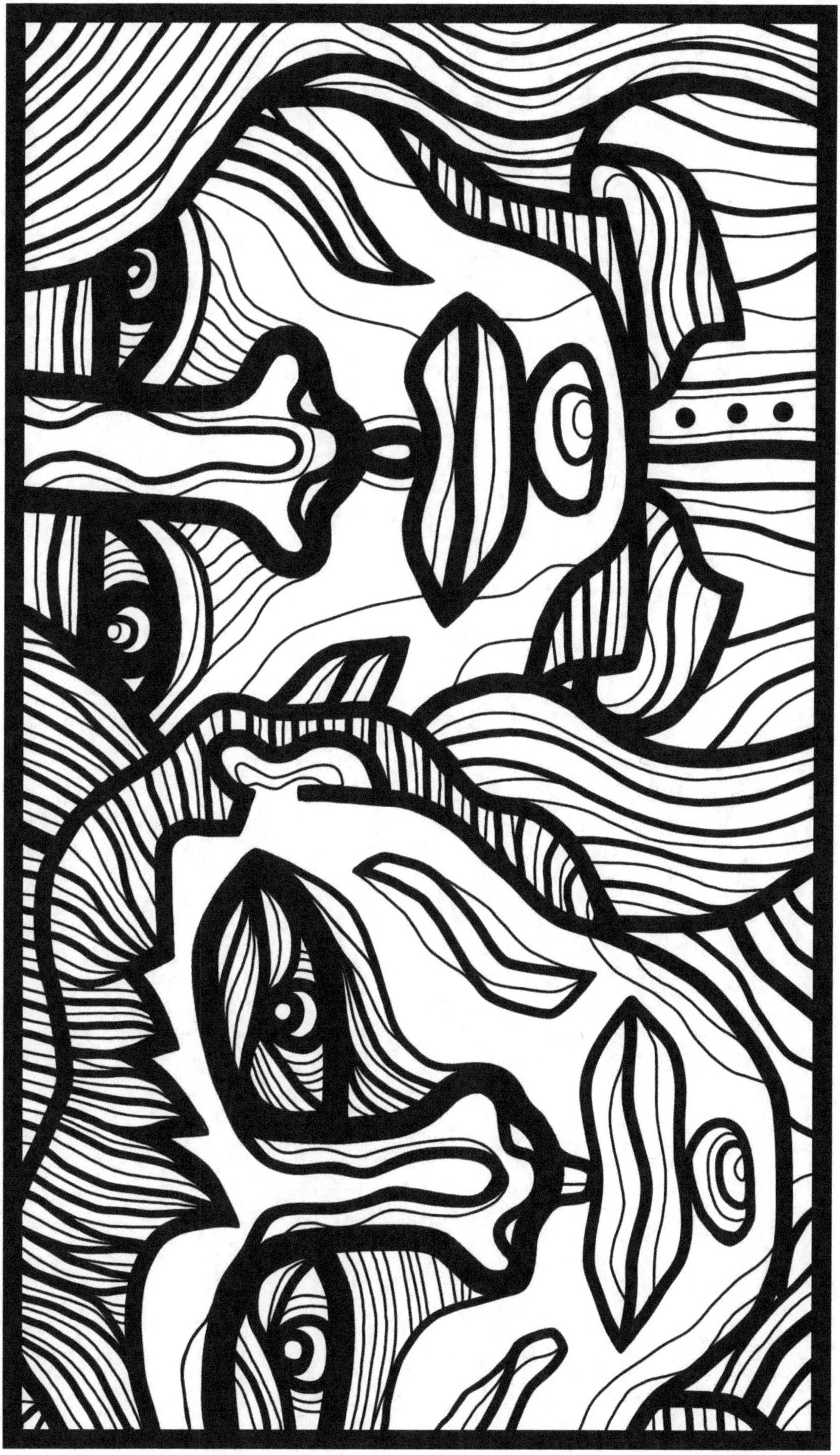

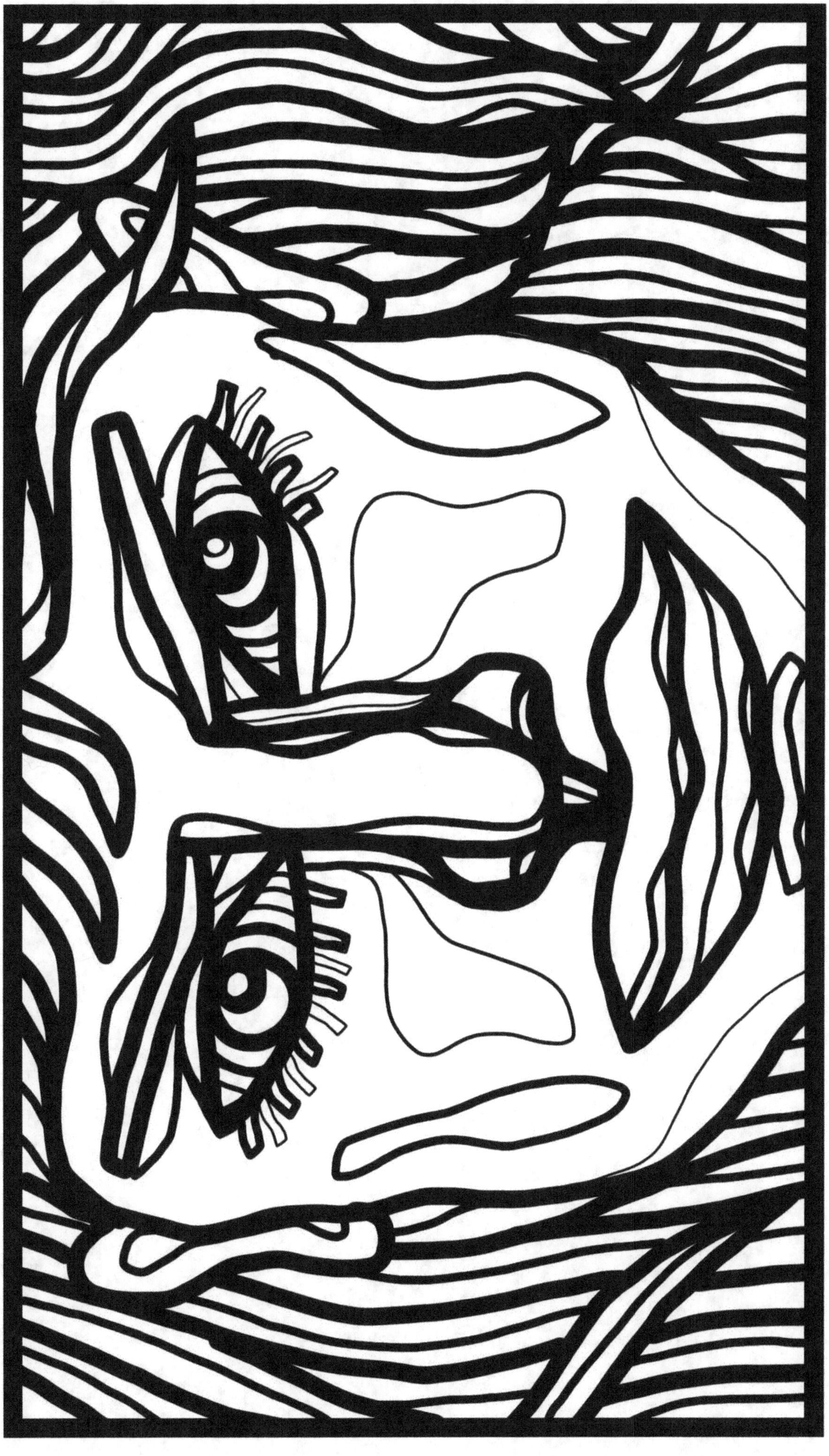

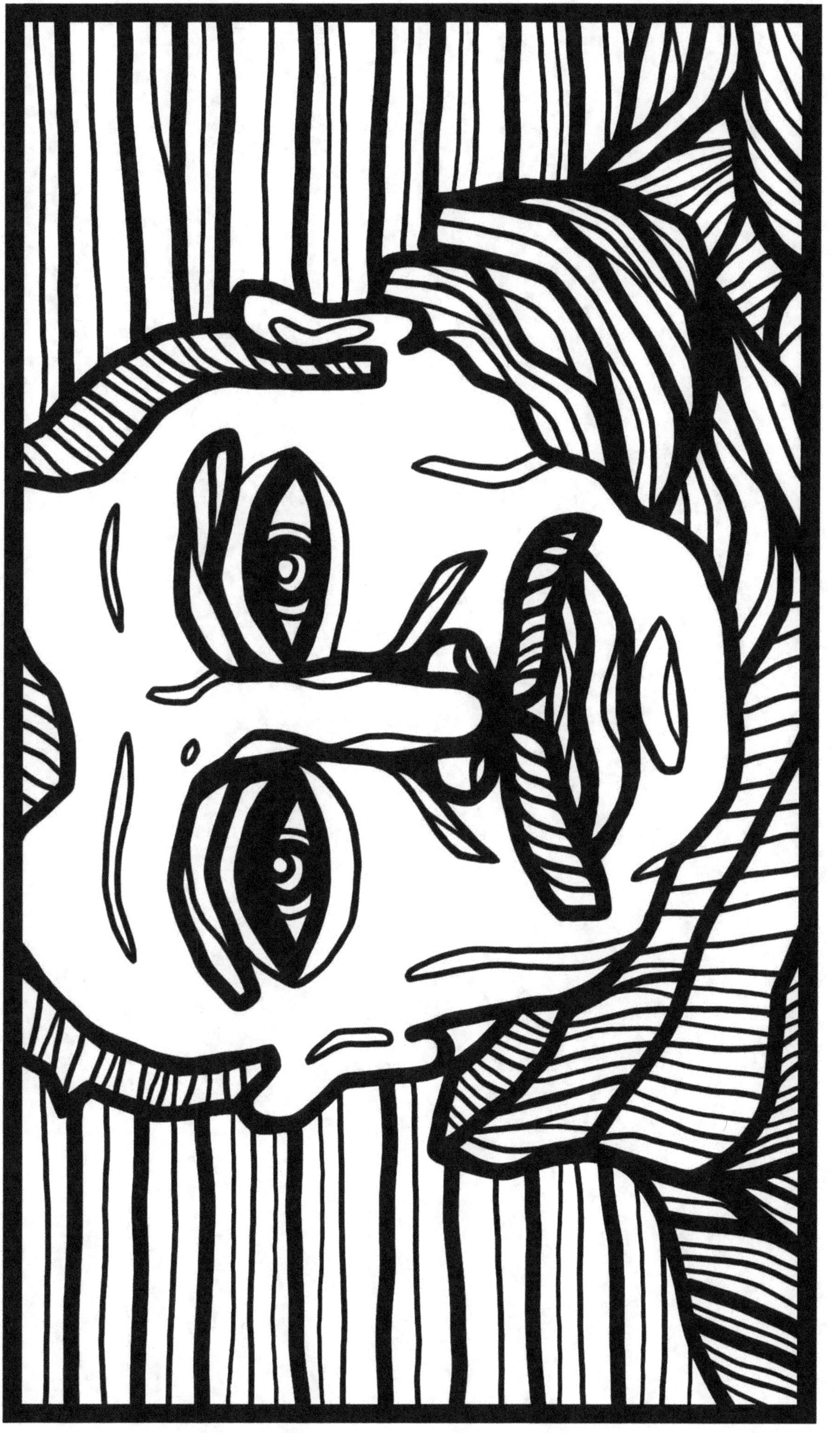

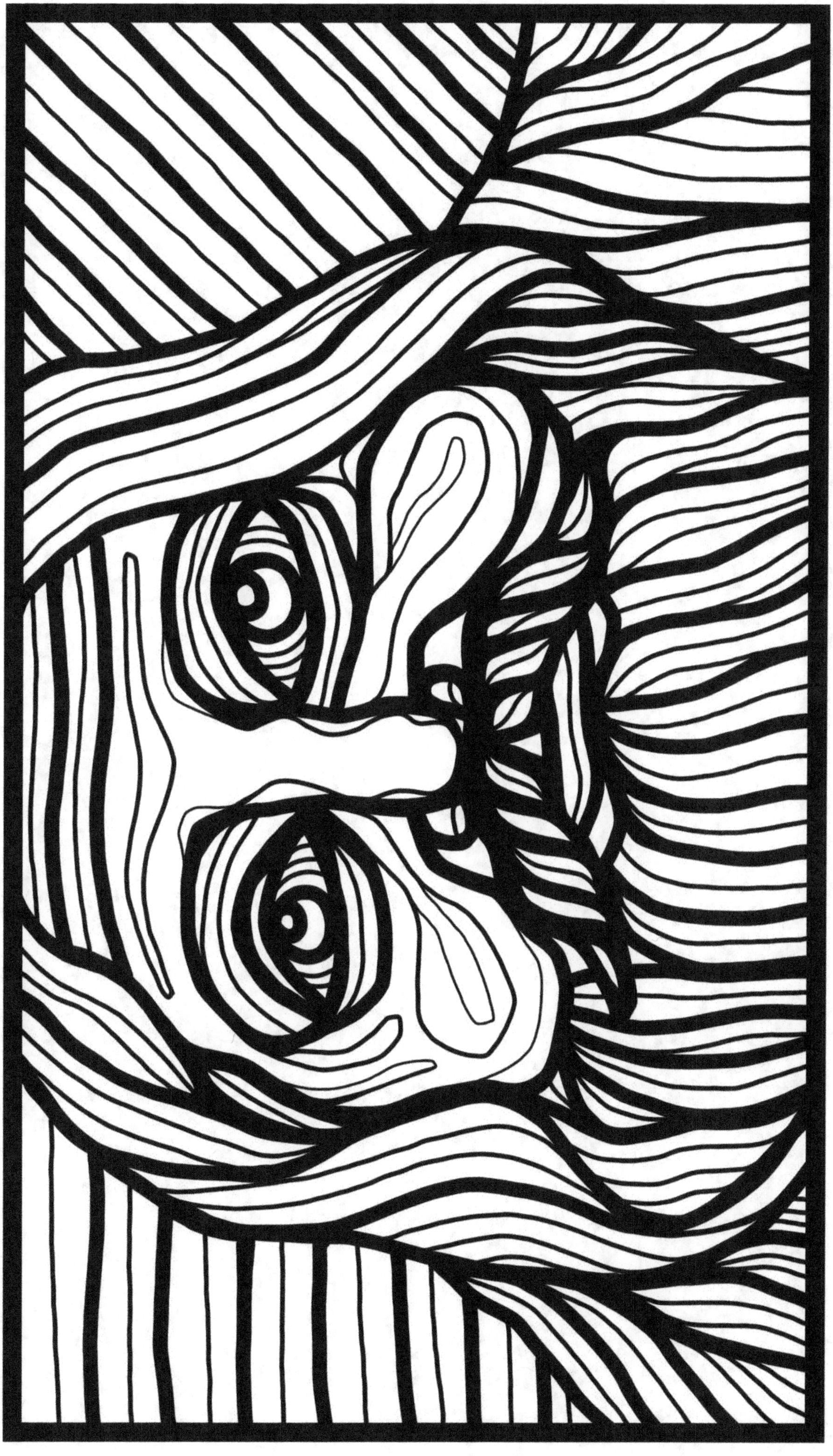

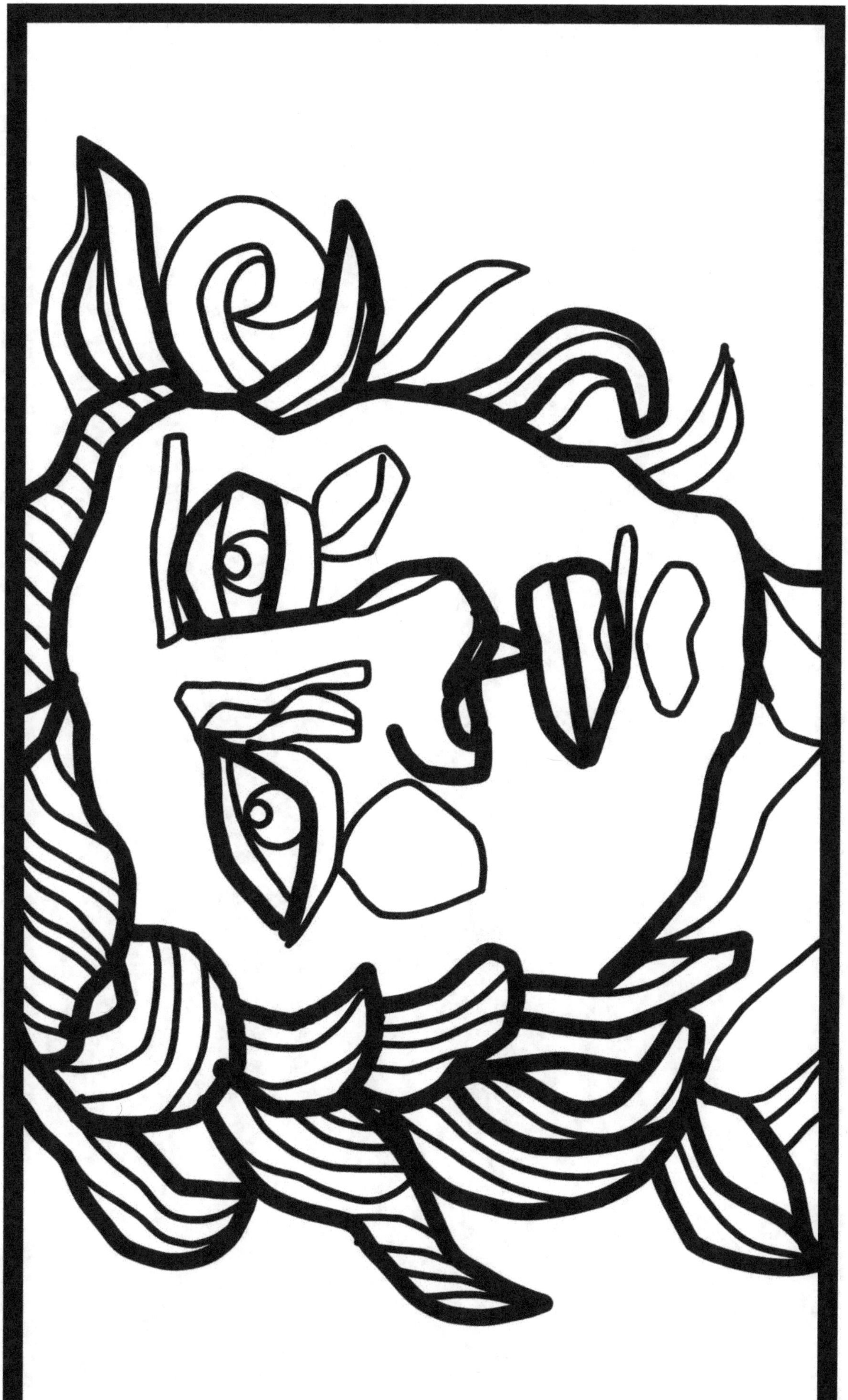

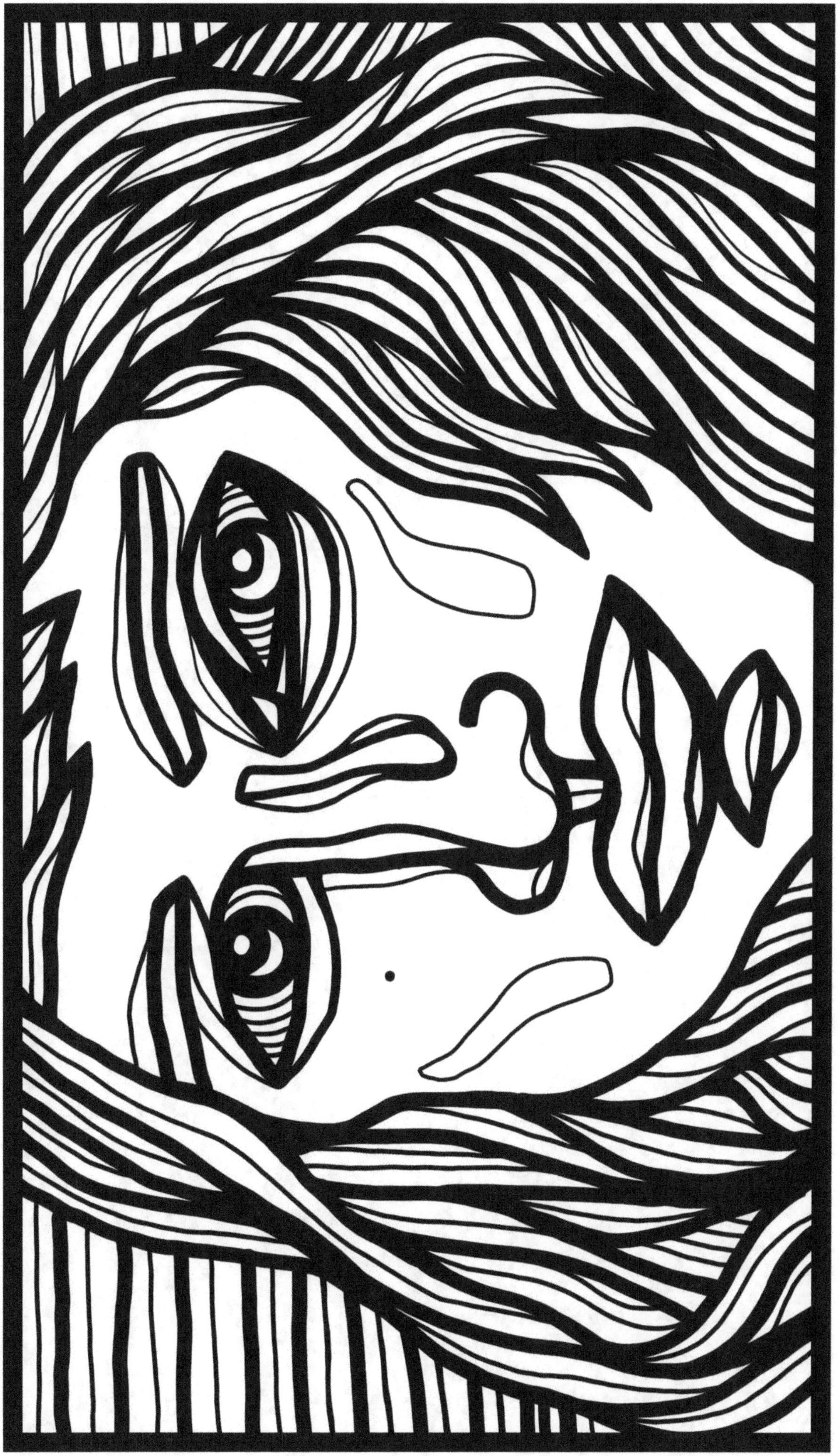

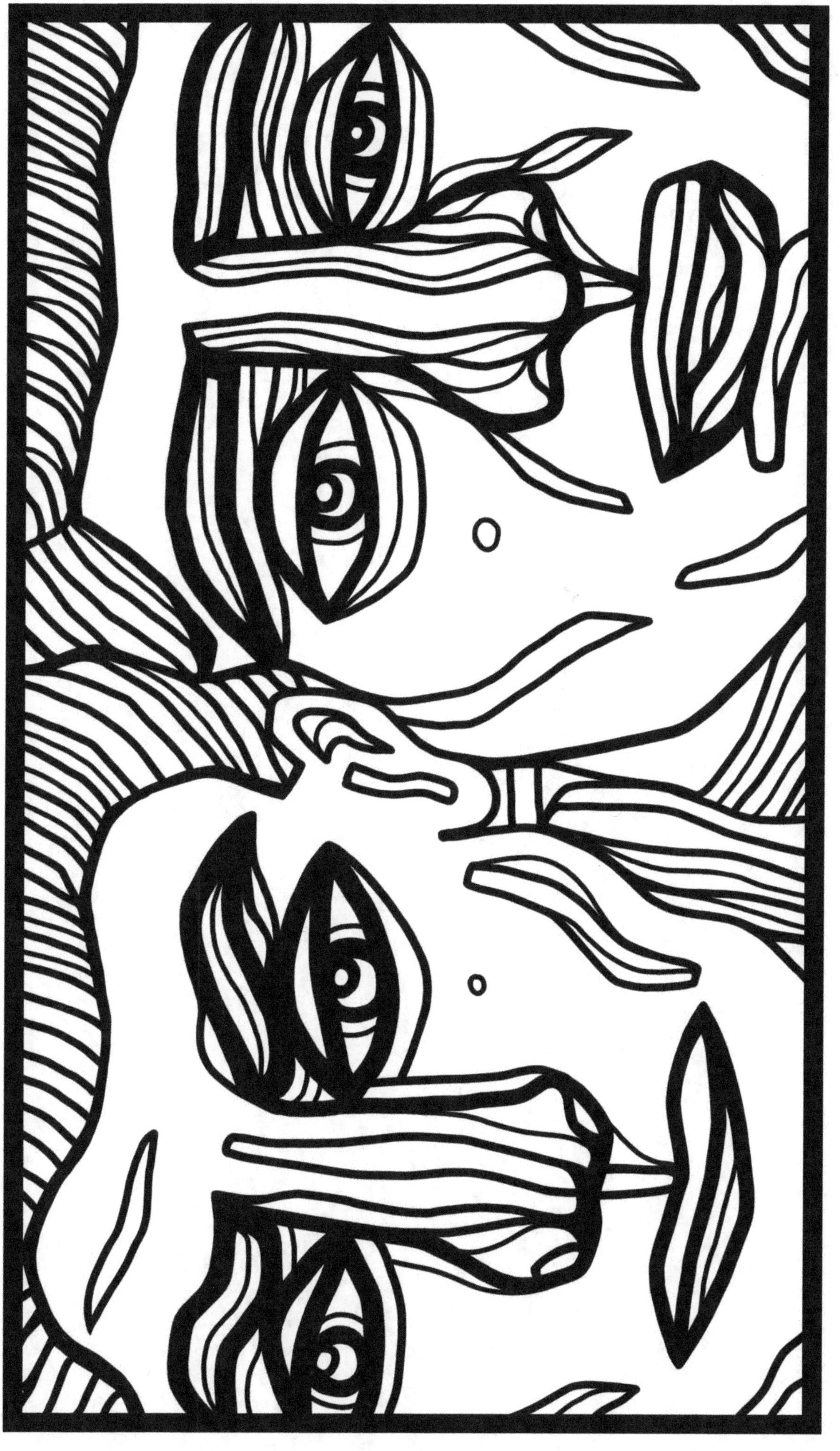

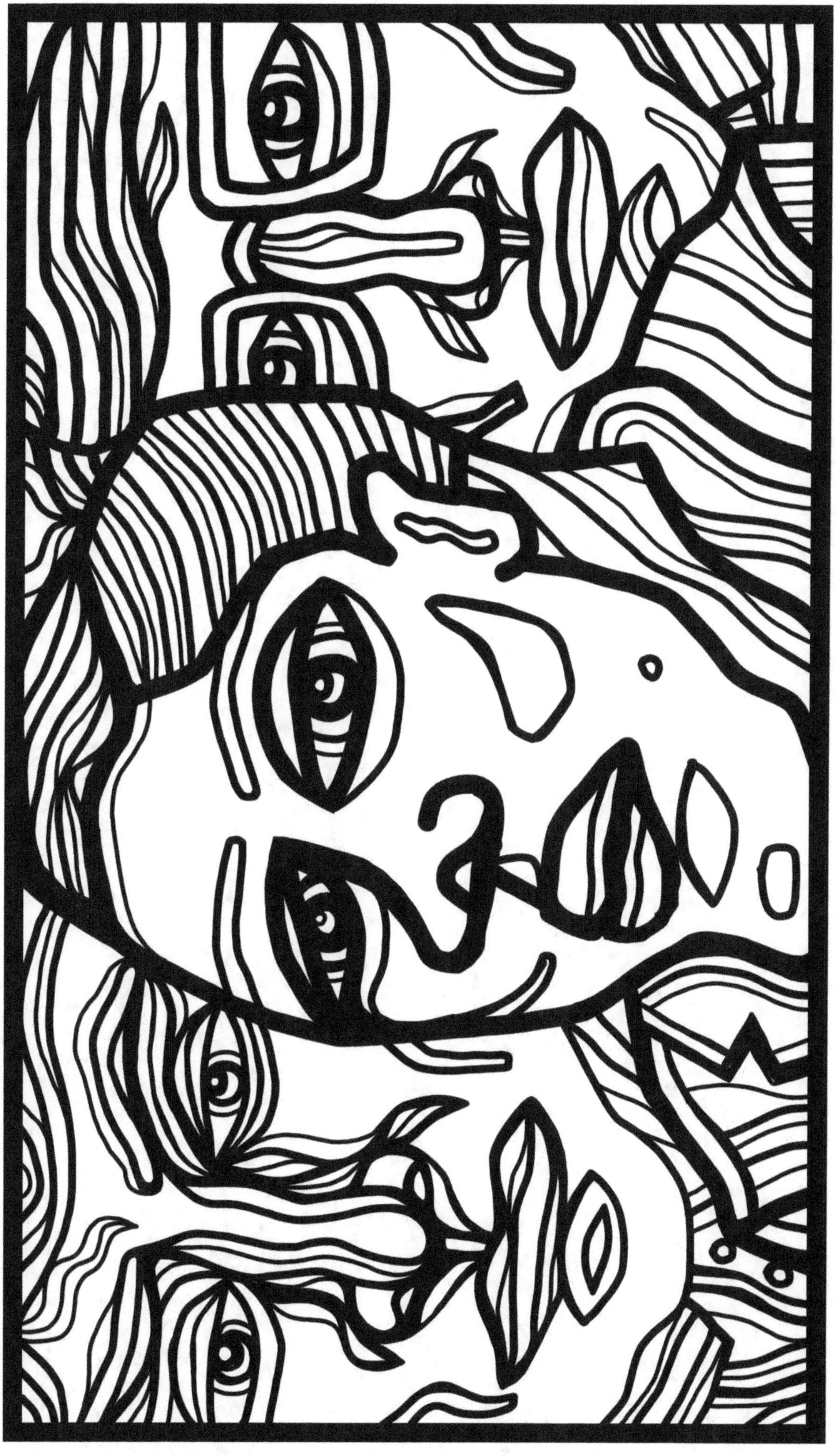

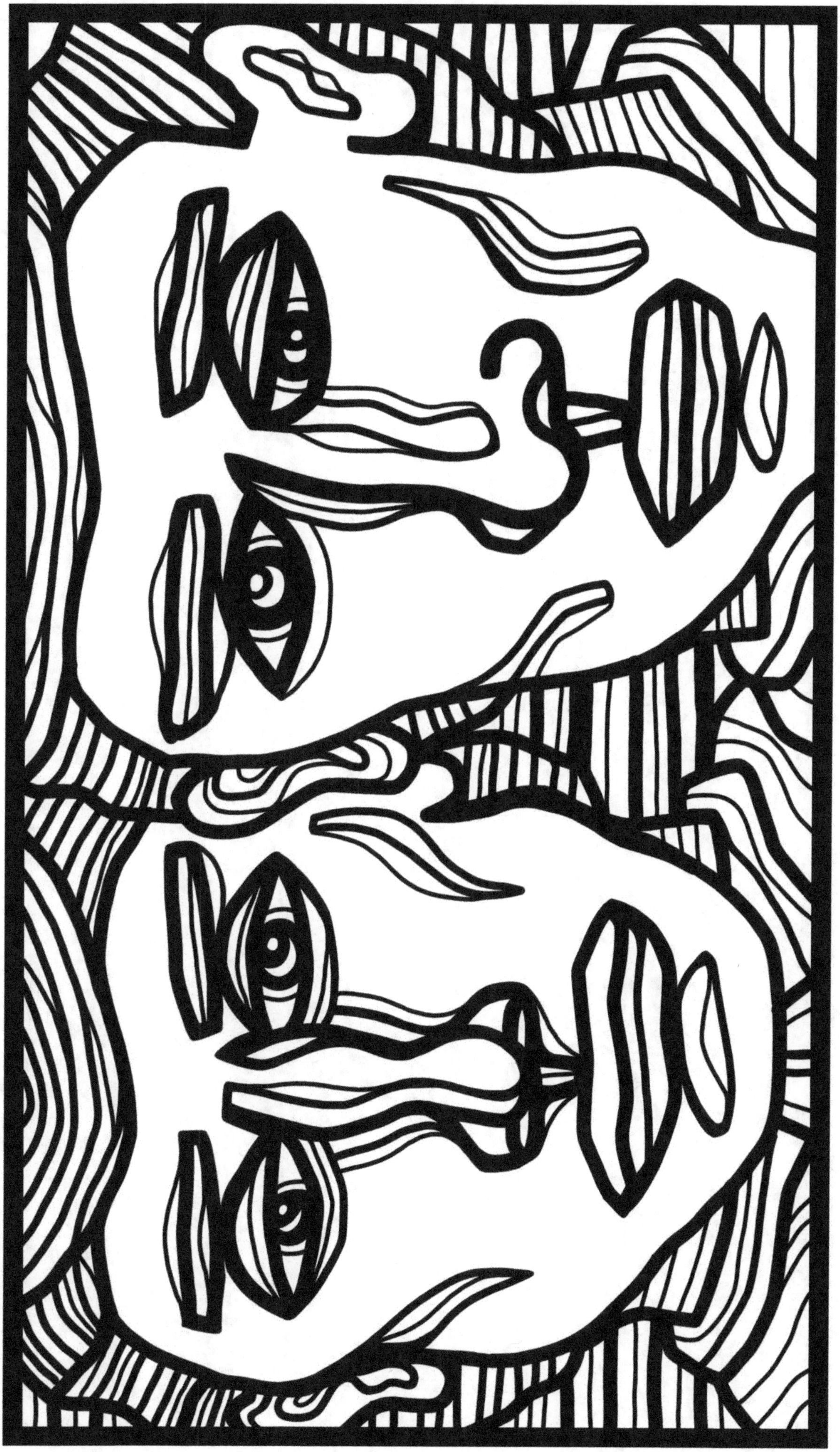

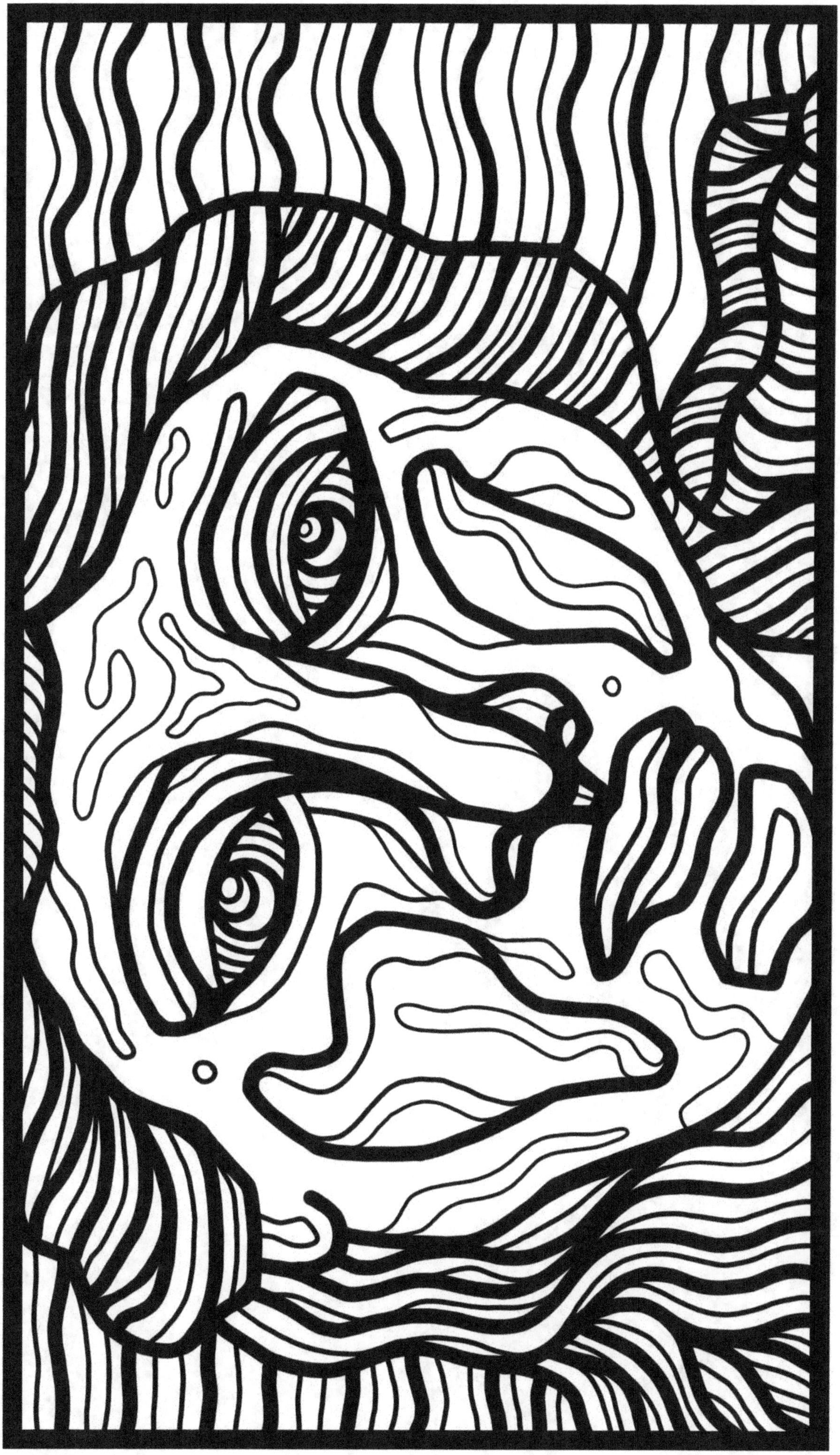

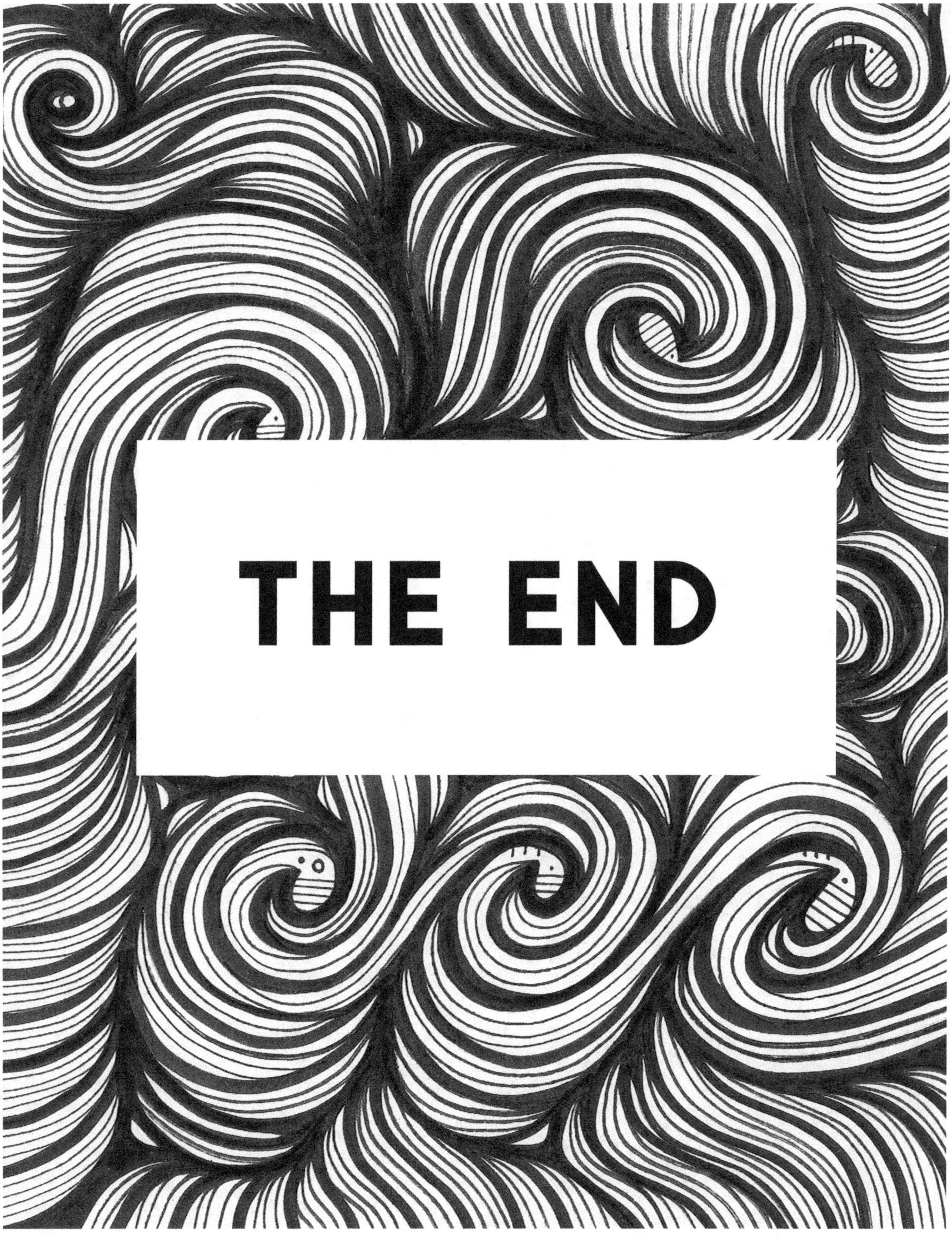
THE END

ART BY:

EDDIE ALFARO

SPONSORED BY:

631ART.COM

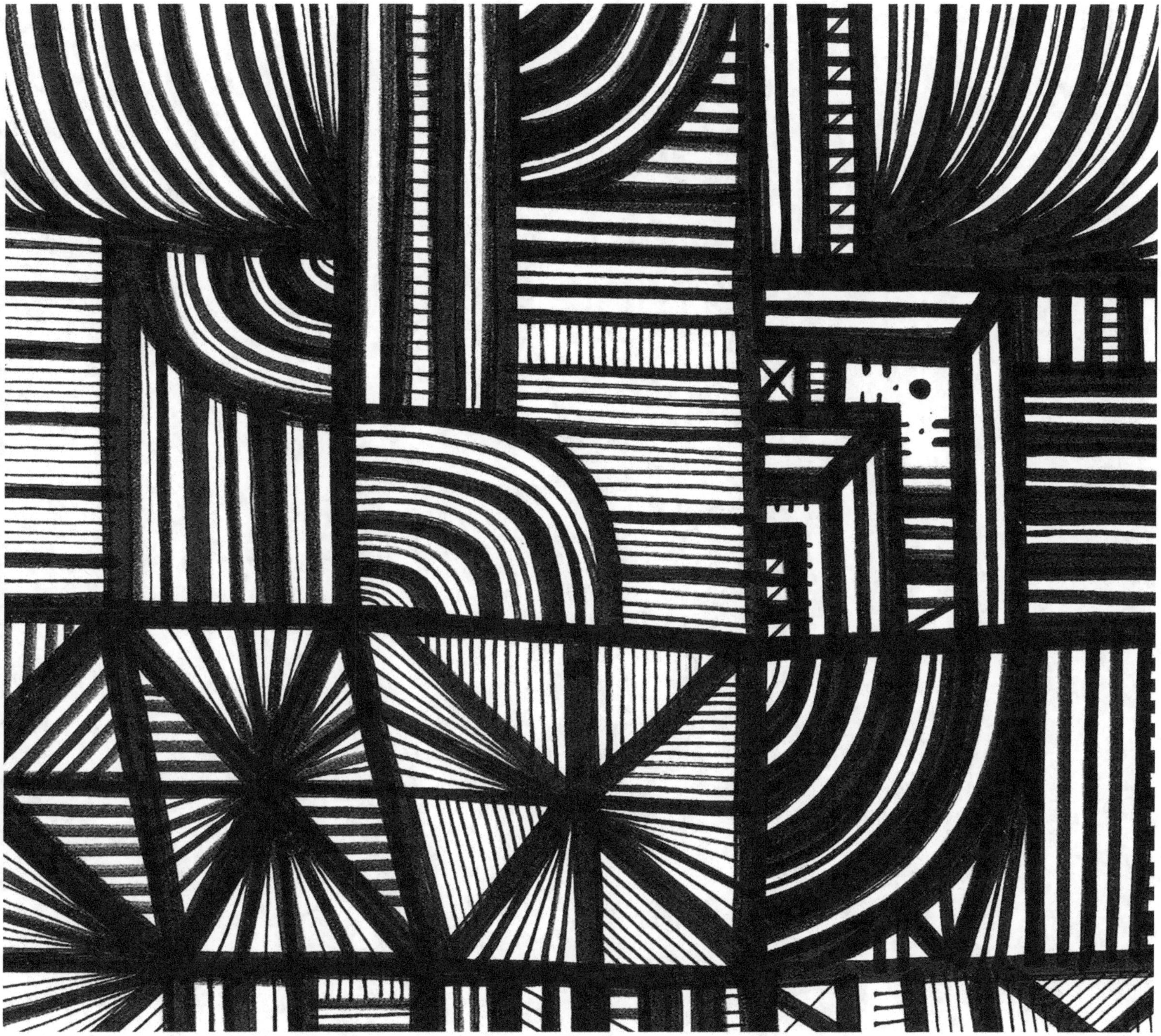

www.ingramcontent.com/pod-product-compliance
Lightning Source LLC
Chambersburg PA
CBHW080130240526
45468CB00009BA/2335
* 9 7 8 1 7 9 5 5 9 9 5 4 2 *